KU-166-230

MEDICINE

A MAGNIFICENTLY ILLUSTRATED
HISTORY

BRIONY HUDSON

NICK TAYLOR

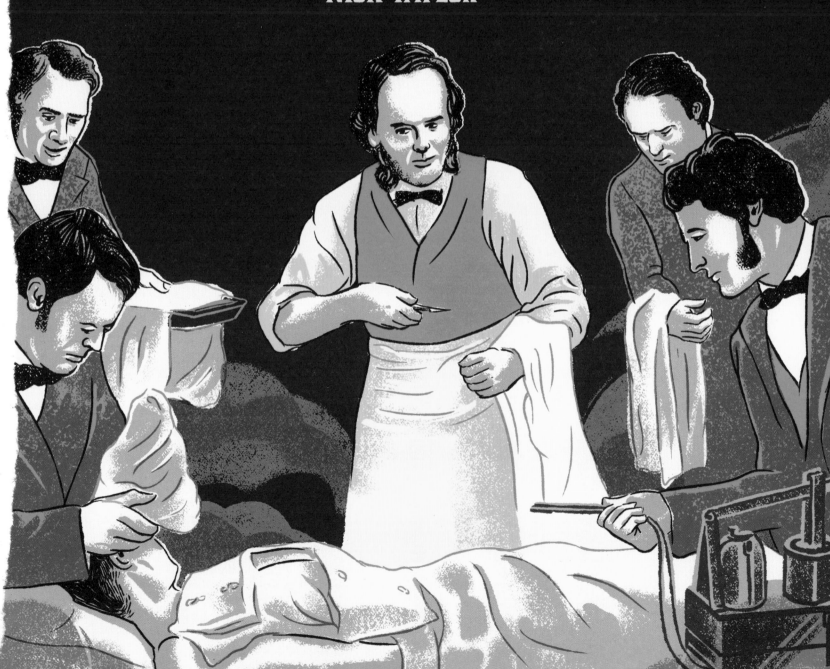

For Lucy, Ava and Zoe – B.H.

Thanks to Kerri, mum and my friends and family for their unerring support.
This book is dedicated to my dad, Les Taylor, who blessed our lives with extra time thanks to the wonders of medicine. – N.T.

BIG PICTURE PRESS

First published in the UK in 2022 by Big Picture Press,
an imprint of Bonnier Books UK
4th Floor, Victoria House
Bloomsbury Square, London WC1B 4DA
Owned by Bonnier Books
Sveavägen 56, Stockholm, Sweden
www.bonnierbooks.co.uk

Text copyright © 2022 by Briony Hudson
Illustration copyright © 2022 by Nick Taylor
Design copyright © 2022 by Big Picture Press

1 3 5 7 9 10 8 6 4 2

All rights reserved

ISBN 978-1-78741-937-7

This book was typeset in Veneer and Bahnscrift
The illustrations were created digitally

Designed by Olivia Cook and Winsome d'Abreu
Edited by Joanna McInerney and Victoria Garrard
Fact checking by Ross MacFarlane
Production by Emma Kidd

With special thanks to Selina Hurley, Natasha McEnroe
and Anne Stobart

Printed in Latvia

MIX
Paper | Supporting
responsible forestry
FSC
www.fsc.org
FSC® C002795

MEDICINE

A MAGNIFICENTLY ILLUSTRATED
HISTORY

BRIONY HUDSON
NICK TAYLOR

BPP

CONTENTS

THE HISTORY

BREAKING BOUNDARIES

Dossibai Patell (1881-1960) trained as a doctor in her native Mumbai, India, and continued her medical education in Britain. She was the first woman to gain a licence from the Royal College of Physicians, the first woman to become a member of the Royal College of Surgeons of England, and the first Indian woman to get a Doctor of Medicine degree from the London School of Tropical Medicine. Patell was the first woman to teach at an Indian medical college, and was made an MBE in 1941 for her work for the Red Cross in India during the Second World War.

The history of medicine is the history of everybody – and every *body* – past and present. In many ways, our experiences today are very similar to those of people who lived long ago. Got a headache? Take advice about something that will make you feel better. Broken your leg? Try to numb the pain, while getting help to ensure it heals. But in other ways, today's medical care is very different from that of the past. Scientific understanding of how our bodies work, access to clean hospitals with expert staff and a choice of effective medicines have revolutionised healthcare. Medicine is adapting all the time, with patients and professionals seeking solutions to challenging problems, from new drugs to better communication.

Medical history is not a simple story, although it has sometimes been told that way. In the past, the diseases people caught and the treatments available to them differed depending on where they lived and when, on whether they were wealthy or not, and on details about their identity, including their gender, race and age. Although it can be hard to uncover the evidence, finding out how individual people felt about their experiences is just as important as facts about new techniques and technology.

HEALTHCARE CHOICES

Mary Clarke, who lived in England in the 1600s, took medical advice from many sources for herself, her 11 children and their servants. In letters to her husband, she described using brown paper for bumps and bruises, and dosing her children with rhubarb for swollen faces. She also bought Hungary water (white wine and rosemary) and syrup of roses from the **apothecary**, whose advice she took when her children were unwell. If home or local remedies didn't work, Clarke consulted her family friend the famous **physician** and philosopher John Locke (1632–1704) about the children's ailments, such as a possible case of **rickets**.

OF MEDICINE

Medical history is also global, as people, diseases and ideas move between countries, with positive and negative impact. European colonisers brought terrible diseases into **colonised** countries, and often devalued existing traditional medicines – a legacy that continues today. Inequalities still exist, with medicines and healthcare not available to everyone, but sharing knowledge around the world has also accelerated techniques and technology. **Vaccines** are an impressive example of this, whether it be the global eradication of smallpox, or the rapid development of vaccines for COVID-19.

Medical history not only records progress, but also delves into the complicated stories behind successes and failures. The emphasis has frequently been on individual white, male pioneers, but breakthroughs are often about teamwork and collaboration. As we find out more about the past, historians continue to enrich medical history.

INTERNATIONAL IMPACT

Pedianos Dioscorides, a Greek army physician and plant hunter, was born in Anavarza, now in Turkey, in about 40CE. He wrote a five-volume book, *De materia medica*, recording practical details about 830 medicinal plants, minerals and animals. Translated into many languages, his ideas were shared and added to in the Arab world and Europe for more than 1,500 years.

RICH HISTORIES

Kwasimukamba (1692–1787), an enslaved man from West Africa, was taken to South America by his Dutch owners as a child, and became a successful healer. He earned enough money to buy his freedom, partly owing to his discovery that making a bitter tea from the bark of a local plant effectively treated infections caused by intestinal parasites. Famous botanist Carl Linnaeus (1707–78) later named the plant *Quassia amara* after Kwasimukamba. European people used the bark to treat vomiting and fever, and scientists continue to research its medicinal uses today, including for **diabetes** and malaria.

LEARNING FROM THE PAST

Exploring the lives of people in the past requires detective work. Humans have always suffered illness and injury, but to understand past treatments and beliefs, we need to examine the historical evidence that survives. Everything from skeletons to manuscripts, portraits to songs, can help us to piece together the clues.

UP CLOSE AND PERSONAL

Skeletons and mummies provide a very personal way to investigate medical history. Today, scientists use modern medical techniques to study them and find out as much as they can about the diseases, injuries and diets of the past.

Specialist scientists called osteoarchaeologists research skeletons from many different centuries and have found signs of cancer, plague, **fractures**, vitamin **deficiencies** and tooth decay. Healed bone injuries even provide evidence that early humans successfully kept severe wounds clean.

In mummified bodies, the soft tissue, amazingly, survives. In 1993, scientists discovered the frozen mummified body of a 25-year-old woman in the Altai Mountains in Siberia. An MRI scan (see page 23) showed that she had suffered from breast cancer and a bone infection, and had had significant injuries, perhaps from falling off a horse.

In 1972, archaeologists found fossilised Viking faeces (known as a coprolite) in York, UK. Examination under a microscope shows that it contains pollen grains and bran, but also hundreds of **parasite** eggs, suggesting the person's stomach and intestines would have been full of worms.

WRITTEN RECORDS AND ARTEFACTS

Some of the oldest medical records are around 4,000 years old, created by the Assyrian people who lived in parts of present-day Iraq, Turkey and Iran. They recorded their **prescriptions** and medical recipes on clay tablets using **cuneiform** symbols. Other peoples including Aboriginal Australians and Native Americans passed down medical knowledge through stories and songs.

Before the printing press was invented in the 1400s, books were written and illustrated by hand, and as a result were rare and expensive. As more people learned to read, printed medical books spread information more quickly, but often used complicated expert language which many people could not understand. Today, these sources reveal the beliefs of the people who wrote them, whether that's a handwritten medical recipe from the 16th century, or a textbook about disease from the 19th century.

Archaeologists and **curators** can also use other surviving objects to find out more. For example, ancient Roman surgical instruments look very similar to tools we use today, suggesting that their purpose may not have changed very much. Historians can read Latin labels on ceramic jars to find out what 17th-century apothecaries sold to their customers.

EVOLVING PERCEPTIONS

Examining historical evidence uncovers people's past medical beliefs, and while surviving sources provide many different perspectives, there are still lots of gaps in our knowledge. Our interpretation also changes over time. For example, an 18th-century painting of a tooth worm shows that people at the time believed that this was responsible for rotting teeth. Today we know that a worm is not the cause. Researchers are constantly finding new evidence, so who knows what we might discover next?

ANCIENT BELIEFS

Humans have always looked for ways to cure illnesses and treat injuries, but ideas and beliefs have changed over time. Today, if we feel ill or have an injury we often turn to medical treatments, but there are lots of other traditions which have historically made people feel better.

FAITH AND HOPE

In many past cultures, how you were feeling was believed to depend on the gods, the stars or luck. Linking body parts and diseases with the position of the stars, moon and planets is a practice used all over the world. In fact, the word influenza, which we often shorten to 'flu', comes from the Italian word for 'influence' of the planets. In medieval Europe, doctors linked each part of the body to an astrological sign (such as Pisces for the feet) and treatment was only carried out when the stars were in the correct position.

THE POWER OF TRUST

Kings and queens were once believed to have a God-given power to cure the disease **scrofula**. From the 11th–17th centuries, people queued to be touched by a monarch, or wore a coin around their neck which had been touched by royalty. Patients taking a **placebo** can often feel better, and scientists are still trying to understand the importance of trusting someone or something to provide a cure.

In the Dahomey culture in West Africa, the great creator god had to be happy before medical remedies would work.

Some ancient Greek people made sacrifices or underwent surgery at temples devoted to Asclepius, the god of healing.

Ancient Egyptians called on the lioness-headed goddess Sekhmet to cure disease.

In traditional Australian medicine, good health relies on a person being connected with nature and the land, as well as positive links with spirits and ancestors.

For Native Americans, treatment might start with climbing a sacred mountain.

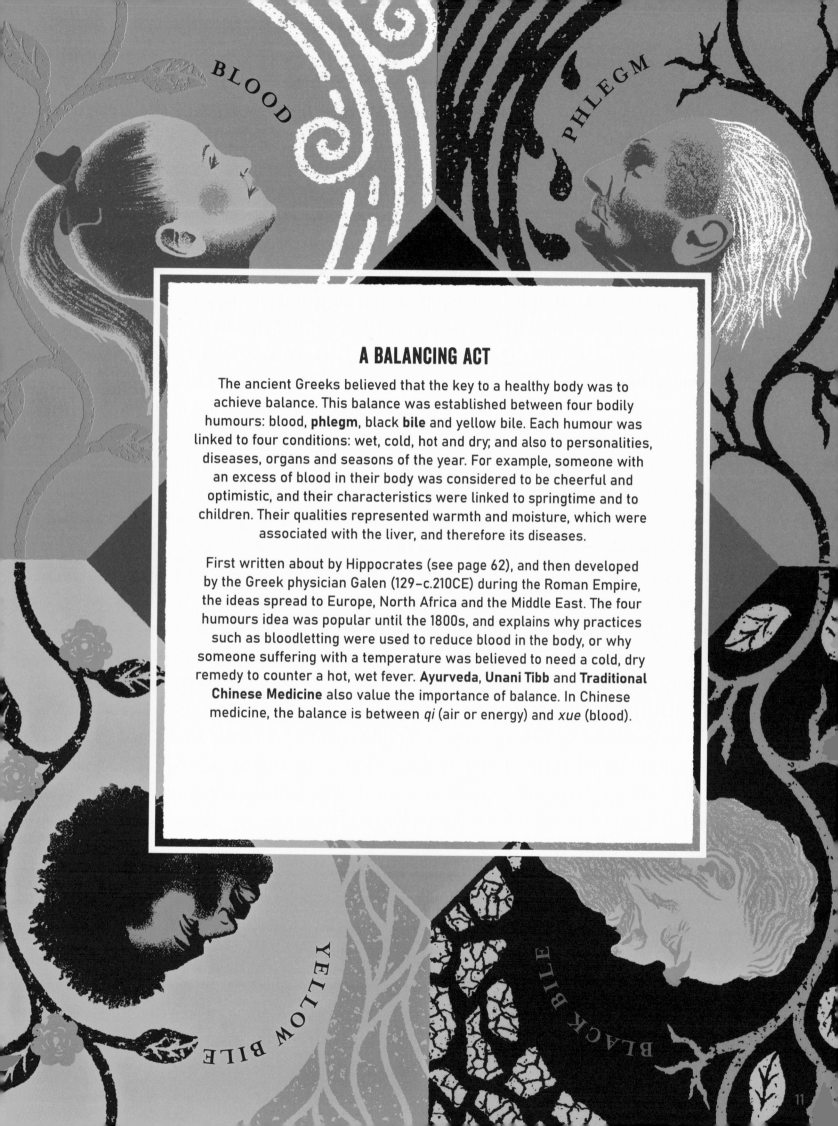

A BALANCING ACT

The ancient Greeks believed that the key to a healthy body was to achieve balance. This balance was established between four bodily humours: blood, **phlegm**, black **bile** and yellow bile. Each humour was linked to four conditions: wet, cold, hot and dry; and also to personalities, diseases, organs and seasons of the year. For example, someone with an excess of blood in their body was considered to be cheerful and optimistic, and their characteristics were linked to springtime and to children. Their qualities represented warmth and moisture, which were associated with the liver, and therefore its diseases.

First written about by Hippocrates (see page 62), and then developed by the Greek physician Galen (129–c.210CE) during the Roman Empire, the ideas spread to Europe, North Africa and the Middle East. The four humours idea was popular until the 1800s, and explains why practices such as bloodletting were used to reduce blood in the body, or why someone suffering with a temperature was believed to need a cold, dry remedy to counter a hot, wet fever. **Ayurveda**, **Unani Tibb** and **Traditional Chinese Medicine** also value the importance of balance. In Chinese medicine, the balance is between *qi* (air or energy) and *xue* (blood).

YELLOW BILE

BLACK BILE

MENTAL HEALTH

Medical history often focuses on the body, but people have suffered with mental illness throughout history too. It wasn't until the 20th century, however, that scientists were better able to understand how the mind works and develop effective treatments. Prior to that, the treatment of the mind was often overlooked and sufferers were regularly treated cruelly or hidden from view. Our knowledge of mental health continues to evolve.

UNDERSTANDING THE MIND

Some doctors in the past explained mental illness using the theory of the four humours (see page 11), with **mania** linked to heat, and **melancholy** linked to excess black bile. From the 1600s, writers such as French philosopher René Descartes (1596–1650) proposed that the mind was separate from the body, which suggested it needed its own specialist doctors. Scientists were also beginning to research the brain's anatomy and how it linked to the body. In the 19th century, doctors formed two new medical specialities: **neurology** – the study of the nervous system; and **psychiatry** – the study of mental illness, behaviours and emotions.

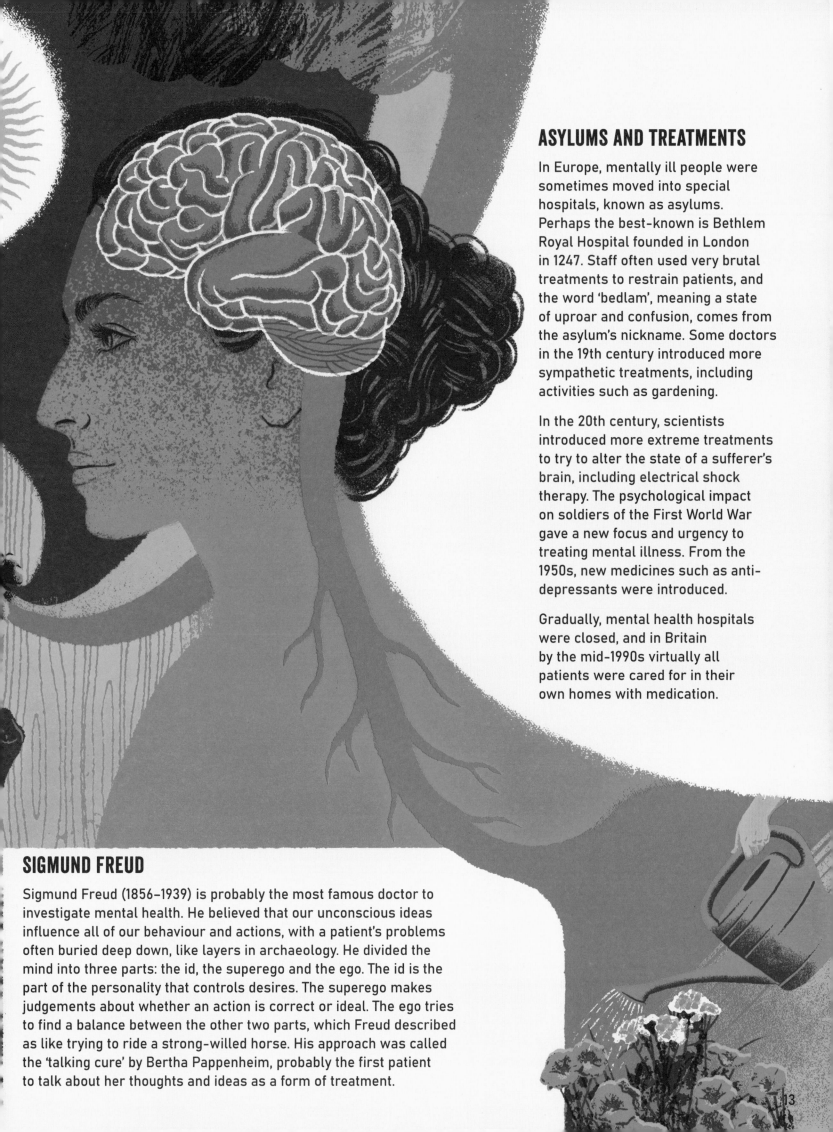

ASYLUMS AND TREATMENTS

In Europe, mentally ill people were sometimes moved into special hospitals, known as asylums. Perhaps the best-known is Bethlem Royal Hospital founded in London in 1247. Staff often used very brutal treatments to restrain patients, and the word 'bedlam', meaning a state of uproar and confusion, comes from the asylum's nickname. Some doctors in the 19th century introduced more sympathetic treatments, including activities such as gardening.

In the 20th century, scientists introduced more extreme treatments to try to alter the state of a sufferer's brain, including electrical shock therapy. The psychological impact on soldiers of the First World War gave a new focus and urgency to treating mental illness. From the 1950s, new medicines such as anti-depressants were introduced.

Gradually, mental health hospitals were closed, and in Britain by the mid-1990s virtually all patients were cared for in their own homes with medication.

SIGMUND FREUD

Sigmund Freud (1856–1939) is probably the most famous doctor to investigate mental health. He believed that our unconscious ideas influence all of our behaviour and actions, with a patient's problems often buried deep down, like layers in archaeology. He divided the mind into three parts: the id, the superego and the ego. The id is the part of the personality that controls desires. The superego makes judgements about whether an action is correct or ideal. The ego tries to find a balance between the other two parts, which Freud described as like trying to ride a strong-willed horse. His approach was called the 'talking cure' by Bertha Pappenheim, probably the first patient to talk about her thoughts and ideas as a form of treatment.

HOW MEDICINES WORK

For generations, humans have noticed that plants such as willow or poppies and substances such as metals and salts affect the body. In more recent history, scientists' growing knowledge about what causes diseases, coupled with how medicines affect our bodies, has dramatically increased the success of medicines. Today, they can improve symptoms such as pain or indigestion, or stop bacteria or viruses from causing infections.

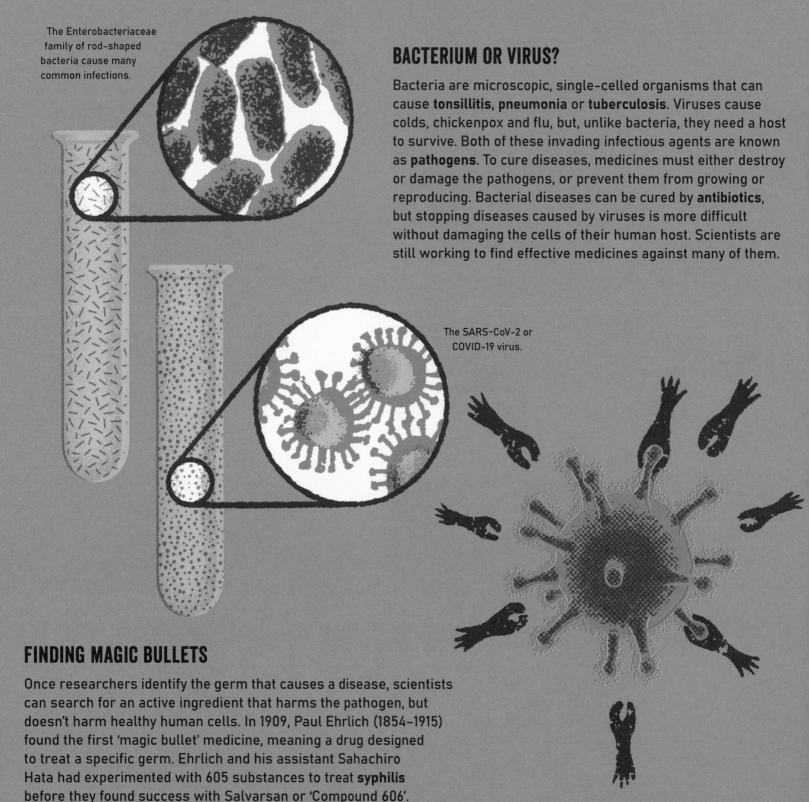

The Enterobacteriaceae family of rod-shaped bacteria cause many common infections.

The SARS-CoV-2 or COVID-19 virus.

BACTERIUM OR VIRUS?

Bacteria are microscopic, single-celled organisms that can cause **tonsillitis**, **pneumonia** or **tuberculosis**. Viruses cause colds, chickenpox and flu, but, unlike bacteria, they need a host to survive. Both of these invading infectious agents are known as **pathogens**. To cure diseases, medicines must either destroy or damage the pathogens, or prevent them from growing or reproducing. Bacterial diseases can be cured by **antibiotics**, but stopping diseases caused by viruses is more difficult without damaging the cells of their human host. Scientists are still working to find effective medicines against many of them.

FINDING MAGIC BULLETS

Once researchers identify the germ that causes a disease, scientists can search for an active ingredient that harms the pathogen, but doesn't harm healthy human cells. In 1909, Paul Ehrlich (1854–1915) found the first 'magic bullet' medicine, meaning a drug designed to treat a specific germ. Ehrlich and his assistant Sahachiro Hata had experimented with 605 substances to treat **syphilis** before they found success with Salvarsan or 'Compound 606'.

GERM THEORY ESTABLISHED ...

Before the 1860s, most people believed that diseases came from the body itself or from bad smells known as miasmas. French scientist Louis Pasteur (1822–95) was among the first to dispel these theories. He discovered that germs or micro-organisms could invade a substance or a body and affect it. Pasteur moved from researching how tiny living particles in wine and milk made them turn sour, to investigating how different germs cause different diseases. He went on to invent the first vaccine against **rabies**, by manipulating the strength of the virus to stop animals and people catching it.

... AND PROVED

German scientist Robert Koch (1843–1910) was inspired by Pasteur, but the two were also rivals. Over an incredibly productive 20-year period, Koch and his students managed to identify and isolate the specific bacteria that caused an impressive range of diseases: **anthrax**, **botulism**, **cholera**, **diphtheria**, **dysentery**, syphilis, **tetanus**, tuberculosis and **typhoid fever**. Pasteur's and Koch's achievements stimulated many more scientists to join the rapidly growing specialism of microbiology, continuing to find ways of preventing the spread of disease.

ETHICS

Medical history doesn't just record successes and miraculous cures. It also records the complex decisions that people have taken in the past or mistakes that have been made. Often, breakthroughs have come at a cost, or are in conflict with the values that we hold today.

THALIDOMIDE

Although new medicines usually make a positive differences to people's lives, sometimes things go wrong. In the 1950s, a new medicine called thalidomide was developed as a sleeping pill. It was also given to pregnant women to ease morning sickness symptoms. However, it had not been tested for this and it was found that the drug damaged the development of unborn babies. Within 10 years of its introduction, more than 10,000 babies worldwide were tragically affected by thalidomide. A large number died, and many others were born without fully formed arms and legs. Thalidomide was banned and changes were made to the way that drugs are tested, approved and marketed.

ANIMAL TESTING

To make sure that medicine is safe for humans, it is often tested on animals. Today, the welfare of animals used in testing is carefully considered and researchers have to follow strict rules to reduce the numbers of animals needed and to minimise suffering. Alternative tests such as computer models are also encouraged wherever possible. However, this has not always been the case, and animal testing has been used for centuries. At a time when cutting open humans was forbidden or restricted, dissecting animals was the best alternative. English physician William Harvey (1578-1657), for example, used dogs, eels, crows and even wasps to test his circulation research. Animal testing became much more widespread in the 1800s as a growing number of scientists carried out research on new treatments. The practice proved increasingly controversial, however, and in 1875 in England, the Irish activist Frances Power Cobbe opposed it by forming the Society for the Protection of Animals Liable to **Vivisection**.

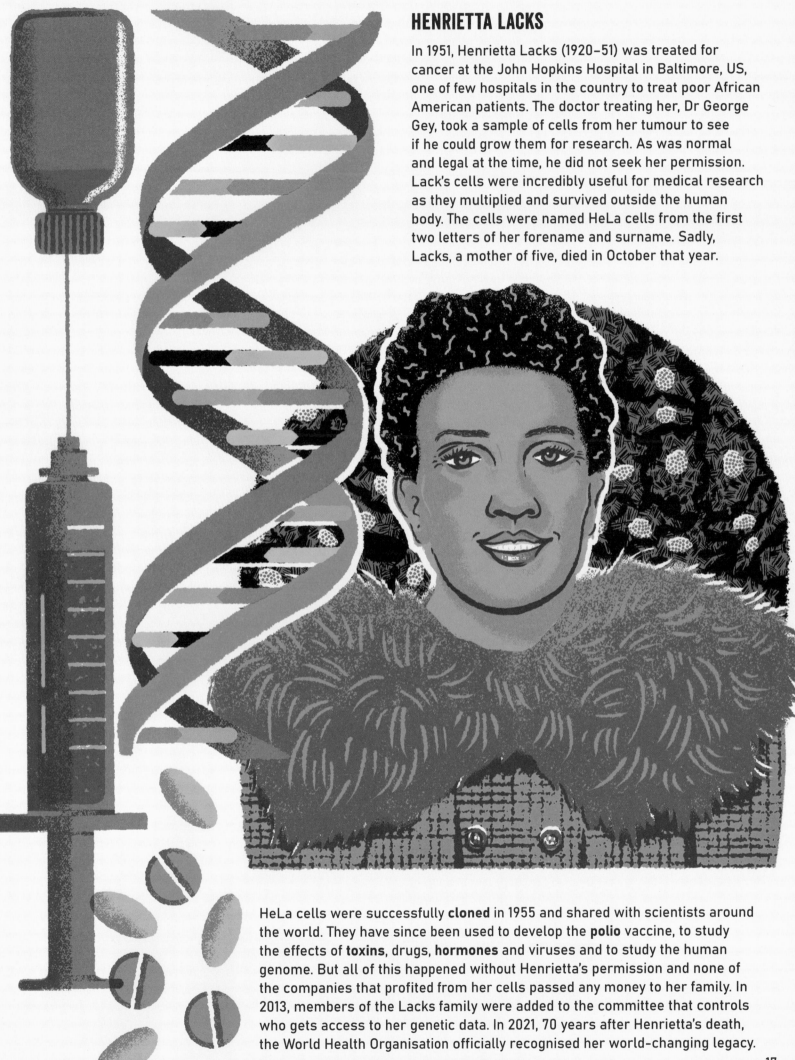

HENRIETTA LACKS

In 1951, Henrietta Lacks (1920–51) was treated for cancer at the John Hopkins Hospital in Baltimore, US, one of few hospitals in the country to treat poor African American patients. The doctor treating her, Dr George Gey, took a sample of cells from her tumour to see if he could grow them for research. As was normal and legal at the time, he did not seek her permission. Lack's cells were incredibly useful for medical research as they multiplied and survived outside the human body. The cells were named HeLa cells from the first two letters of her forename and surname. Sadly, Lacks, a mother of five, died in October that year.

HeLa cells were successfully **cloned** in 1955 and shared with scientists around the world. They have since been used to develop the **polio** vaccine, to study the effects of **toxins**, drugs, **hormones** and viruses and to study the human genome. But all of this happened without Henrietta's permission and none of the companies that profited from her cells passed any money to her family. In 2013, members of the Lacks family were added to the committee that controls who gets access to her genetic data. In 2021, 70 years after Henrietta's death, the World Health Organisation officially recognised her world-changing legacy.

OPENING UP THE BODY

Finding out how the human body works is very difficult unless you can look inside it. The science of 'anatomy' (a term that derives from the ancient Greek for 'to cut up') was vital to a growing understanding of the body's structure. Although the practice is strictly controlled now, people have been dissecting dead bodies for thousands of years.

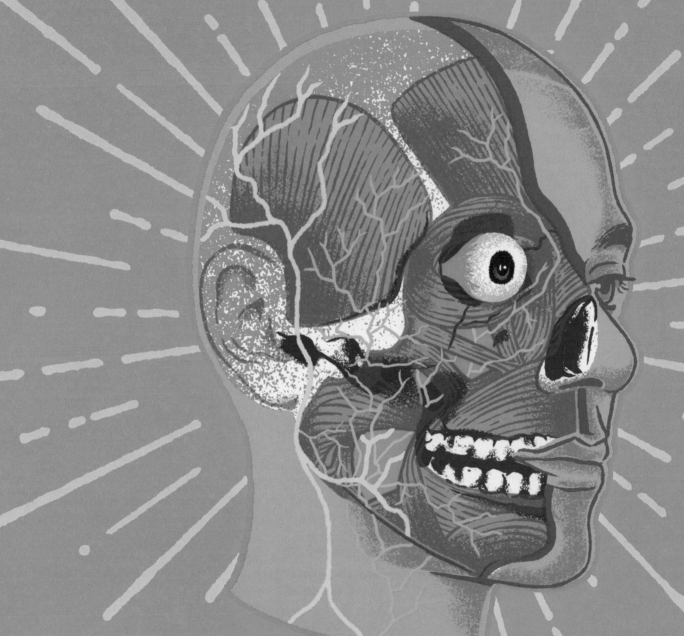

UNDER THE SKIN

Galen, a Greek doctor working in the Roman Empire (see page 11), was revered for his **anatomical** knowledge. He examined human bodies by treating wounded Roman gladiators, but he only carried out dissections on animals which meant that not all of his observations were accurate for humans. For centuries, Galen's work was central to doctors' understanding of anatomy in Islamic countries and in Europe. The first known book from the Islamic world to include anatomical illustrations of the whole body is *Mansur's Anatomy*, written in around 1400. Many people became fascinated by anatomy in the 1500s and Andreas Vesalius (1514–64), professor of anatomy at Padua University in Italy, was especially keen to update Galen's ideas. He published his findings in *De humani corpis fabrica* (On the Fabric of the Human Body) in 1543. This seven-book volume corrected the 300 errors Vesalius had found in Galen's original works.

As medical training developed, there was increasing demand to learn about anatomy from bodies rather than books. By the 1700s, some European universities offered public human anatomy lectures using the corpses of executed criminals. But this limited supply of bodies led to a boom in grave-robbings by unscrupulous types keen to make money. The most infamous 'body snatchers' were William Burke and William Hare in Edinburgh. Although the two never actually robbed a grave, they murdered at least 16 people in 1827 and 1828. Something clearly had to be done. In 1832, the British government passed the Anatomy Act to allow medical schools to use bodies that were unclaimed by their families. Anatomy is still vitally important for medical training today and most doctors carry out human dissection as part of their course. Laws such as the Human Tissue Act in Britain control their ethical use.

MEASURING THE BODY

If doctors are unable to see inside a patient's body, they need other ways to find out what is going on. Since ancient times, doctors have monitored a patient's pulse, observed their temperature and examined their urine to assess their health. Today, they might also take more specific measurements such as checking cardiac enzyme levels for the heart. Many tests have only become widespread and practical with recent developments in both technology and equipment.

READING VITAL SIGNS

For centuries, doctors have examined the appearance and even the taste of a patient's urine as an indication of their health. Ancient physicians such as Hippocrates and Galen linked bodily fluids to the balance of a person's humours (see page 11), and Ibn Sina recorded that some patients' urine evaporated to leave a sweet residue like honey, something we now know to be a symptom of diabetes (see page 73). Today, urine analysis is still used to detect conditions such as diabetes and for pregnancy tests.

HEART AND BLOOD

Although monitoring a patient's heart by taking their pulse has been practised for centuries in many civilisations, counting the pulse accurately is not as easy as it might sound.

Italian physician Sanctorius (1561–1636) introduced a pendulum to help him determine pulse rates, and British doctor Sir John Floyer (1649–1734) added a second hand to a watch to make counting easier.

Recording the pulse rate automatically and accurately on a machine was a significant breakthrough. By the 19th century, German **physiologist** Karl Vierordt (1818–84) had invented the sphygmograph to trace a patient's pulse onto a graph.

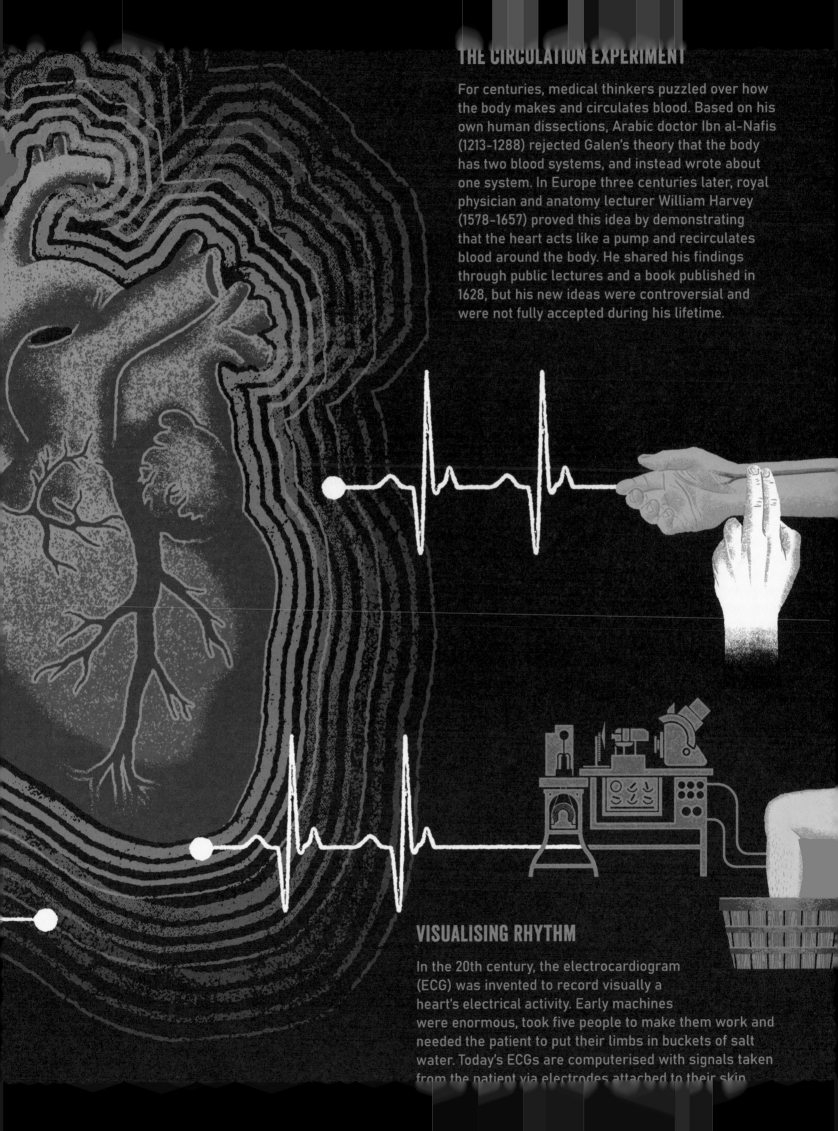

THE CIRCULATION EXPERIMENT

For centuries, medical thinkers puzzled over how the body makes and circulates blood. Based on his own human dissections, Arabic doctor Ibn al-Nafis (1213-1288) rejected Galen's theory that the body has two blood systems, and instead wrote about one system. In Europe three centuries later, royal physician and anatomy lecturer William Harvey (1578-1657) proved this idea by demonstrating that the heart acts like a pump and recirculates blood around the body. He shared his findings through public lectures and a book published in 1628, but his new ideas were controversial and were not fully accepted during his lifetime.

VISUALISING RHYTHM

In the 20th century, the electrocardiogram (ECG) was invented to record visually a heart's electrical activity. Early machines were enormous, took five people to make them work and needed the patient to put their limbs in buckets of salt water. Today's ECGs are computerised with signals taken from the patient via electrodes attached to their skin.

FROM THE INSIDE OUT

For centuries, doctors and scientists rarely got the opportunity to see inside the human body. To be able to work out why a person felt sick, whether they had a more serious disease or how to heal a complicated broken bone was very difficult until scientists developed the equipment we have today.

STETHOSCOPE

In 1816, French doctor René Laennec (1781-1826) invented the stethoscope. Doctors knew that listening to a person's heart, their breathing or the sounds that their digestive system made helped reveal what was going on inside. Laennec's invention meant that they could hear more clearly, and without awkwardly putting their ear on a patient's chest.

The first stethoscopes were simply tubes, before the 'two-eared' type we recognise today was invented in the 1850s. Simple trumpet-shaped tubes are still often used to hear a baby growing in a mother's womb.

X-RAYS

In 1895, German scientist Wilhelm Röntgen (1845-1923) discovered that the rays he was investigating could produce an image of the bones in his hand. He called his discovery X-rays. For the first time, doctors could see inside a living human being without having to cut them open. One of the first images he took was of his wife Anna Bertha Ludwig's hand. In 1901 he was awarded the first ever Nobel Prize in physics for his work.

In their early days, X-rays were a very exciting development, but the dangerous effects of the radiation that make the images possible was not fully understood. Today, we know much more about radiation and safe levels of exposure. Radiation therapy can also treat diseases like cancer.

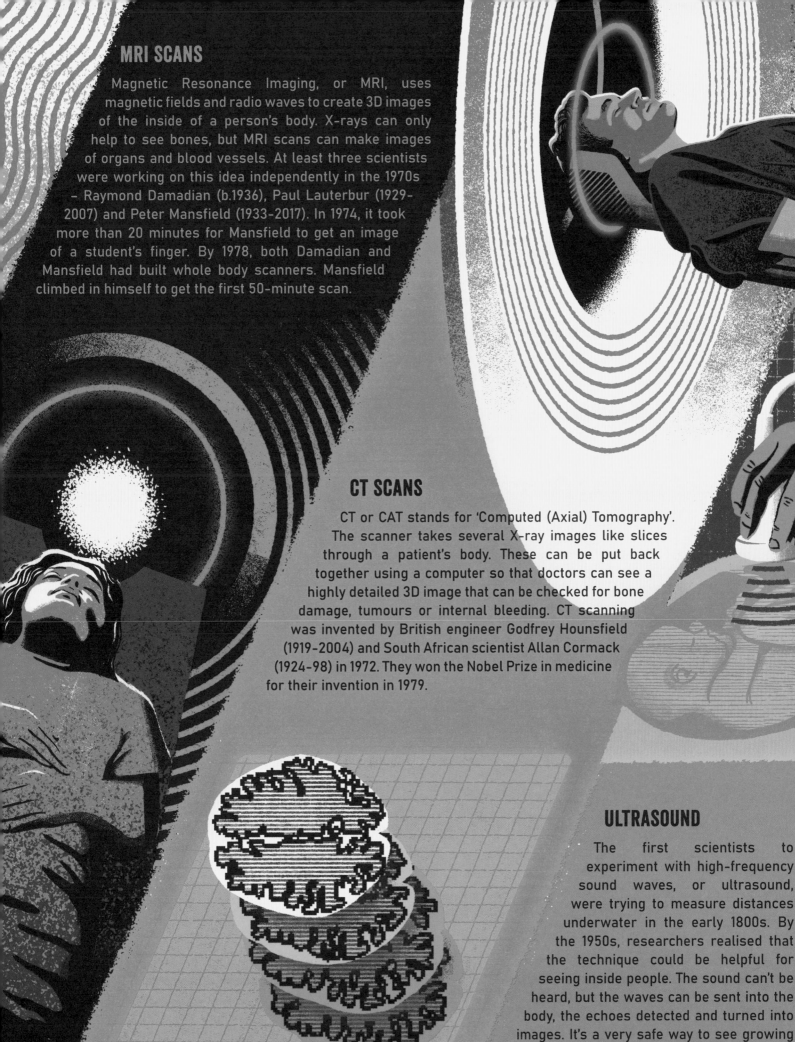

MRI SCANS

Magnetic Resonance Imaging, or MRI, uses magnetic fields and radio waves to create 3D images of the inside of a person's body. X-rays can only help to see bones, but MRI scans can make images of organs and blood vessels. At least three scientists were working on this idea independently in the 1970s – Raymond Damadian (b.1936), Paul Lauterbur (1929-2007) and Peter Mansfield (1933-2017). In 1974, it took more than 20 minutes for Mansfield to get an image of a student's finger. By 1978, both Damadian and Mansfield had built whole body scanners. Mansfield climbed in himself to get the first 50-minute scan.

CT SCANS

CT or CAT stands for 'Computed (Axial) Tomography'. The scanner takes several X-ray images like slices through a patient's body. These can be put back together using a computer so that doctors can see a highly detailed 3D image that can be checked for bone damage, tumours or internal bleeding. CT scanning was invented by British engineer Godfrey Hounsfield (1919-2004) and South African scientist Allan Cormack (1924-98) in 1972. They won the Nobel Prize in medicine for their invention in 1979.

ULTRASOUND

The first scientists to experiment with high-frequency sound waves, or ultrasound, were trying to measure distances underwater in the early 1800s. By the 1950s, researchers realised that the technique could be helpful for seeing inside people. The sound can't be heard, but the waves can be sent into the body, the echoes detected and turned into images. It's a very safe way to see growing babies inside a pregnant woman.

AT A TINY LEVEL

Understanding how our bodies work, how to treat diseases and how medicines work goes further than anatomy. Scientists need to find out what is happening at a cellular level and even smaller. This is only possible with the development of technology to help researchers and doctors.

MICROSCOPES

No one is sure who invented the first microscope. Dutch spectacle maker Zacharias Janssen (born 1585) claims to have made a compound microscope with two lenses in around 1600 which meant that an object could be magnified up to 30 times its actual size. In the 1660s, Antonie van Leeuwenhoek (1632-1723) made simple microscopes with one lens, similar to a magnifying glass, able to magnify an object up to 200 times. He enthusiastically examined animal and plant tissue, blood cells, minerals and fossils and presented his findings to the Royal Society in London, where scientist Robert Hooke (1635-1703) was also making similar discoveries.

Scientists grappled with blurred microscope images and inaccurate colour until manufacturers added mirrors for increased light and higher-quality lenses in the 1800s. These improvements meant that researchers like Pasteur (see page 15) had the equipment they needed to make significant steps in the understanding of the body and diseases.

In the 20th century, new electron microscopes allowed scientists to see micro-organisms like viruses for the first time, and developments in computer technology have continued to improve the uses to which microscopic images can be put. By combining new surgical techniques with microscope technology, surgeons can carry out detailed and precise microsurgery inside a patient's body.

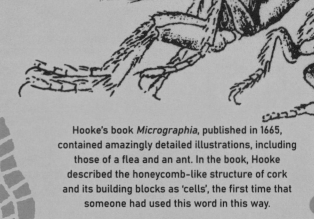

Hooke's book *Micrographia*, published in 1665, contained amazingly detailed illustrations, including those of a flea and an ant. In the book, Hooke described the honeycomb-like structure of cork and its building blocks as 'cells', the first time that someone had used this word in this way.

MOLECULES

In the early 1900s, scientists began to explore other ways to investigate the body's inner workings and the structure of medicinal substances. Dorothy Crowfoot Hodgkin (1910-94) used **X-ray crystallography** to reveal the molecular structure of insulin, penicillin and the newly discovered vitamin B12. She won the Nobel Prize in chemistry in 1964, and remains the only British woman scientist to be honoured in this way. Scientists also used this technique to investigate the structure of proteins, the large molecules that the body uses to build and maintain itself.

DNA is a long molecule that contains each person's unique genetic code (the instructions found inside our chromosomes for making all of our body's proteins).

GENETICS

Meanwhile, researchers were investigating a science that became known as genetics. Czech scientist Gregor Mendel (1822-84) carried out experiments growing pea plants to explore how different characteristics like height and colour were passed through the generations. Scientists discovered that this information was held in the nucleus of cells, which they named chromosomes. In 1905, American scientists Nettie Stevens (1861-1912) and Edmund Wilson (1856-1939) discovered independently that chromosomes determine whether a creature is male or female. We now know that every person inherits a copy of each chromosome from each parent. Understanding their role allows scientists to investigate how different conditions are passed between generations.

In the 1950s, scientists were keen to find out more. British scientist Francis Crick (1916-2004) and American researcher James Watson (born 1928) achieved international fame in 1953 for their discovery of the double-stranded helix structure of deoxyribonucleic acid or DNA.

In 2003, the Human Genome Project successfully sequenced the entire DNA of the human body. This information has made it possible for scientists to develop treatments for diseases which are tailored to individual patients. In the future, it should be possible to sequence a patient's DNA, find out if they are at risk from particular diseases and provide personalised medicines.

THE POWER OF PLANTS

Across the world, researchers estimate that more than 30,000 plant species have been used for medicine – from roots to barks, and from leaves to flowers. People both in the past and today have boiled, crushed, dried and powdered plant materials to take as treatments. Plants have also inspired many modern medicines now produced in laboratories. Aspirin, for example, was inspired by the natural chemicals in willow and meadowsweet.

FROM HEAD TO TOE

Medicinal plants have had different uses over time and between different countries. People across many regions have used senna leaves and seed pods, for example, to treat **constipation**, but in Traditional Chinese Medicine they are also recommended to brighten the eyes, and the Ayurvedic tradition values them in treating **bronchitis** and skin problems. Using plants to heal and treat diseases has always required expert skills. Different parts of plants have different uses and effects on the body, so an exact combination of plants and other ingredients is required.

Pomegranate
Pomegranate juice has been used for centuries to treat mouth and eye infections.

Daffodil
Galantamine from daffodil bulbs and flowers is used to treat **Alzheimer's disease** today.

Lime flower
People in Europe believed that the power of linden (or lime) tree flowers to treat **epilepsy** was so strong that you just needed to sit underneath the tree in order to be cured!

Cucumber
Ancient Roman medical writer Celsus recommended a mixture of vinegar, oil, crushed rose leaves and cucumber juice to remove ear wax.

Ephedra or Ma Huang
This has been used in Chinese medicine since at least 2700BCE for coughs and fevers. The active chemical pseudoephedrine is used today as a decongestant.

Foxglove
This was first used as a medicine in the 1700s. The active chemical digoxin is still an important treatment for heart conditions today.

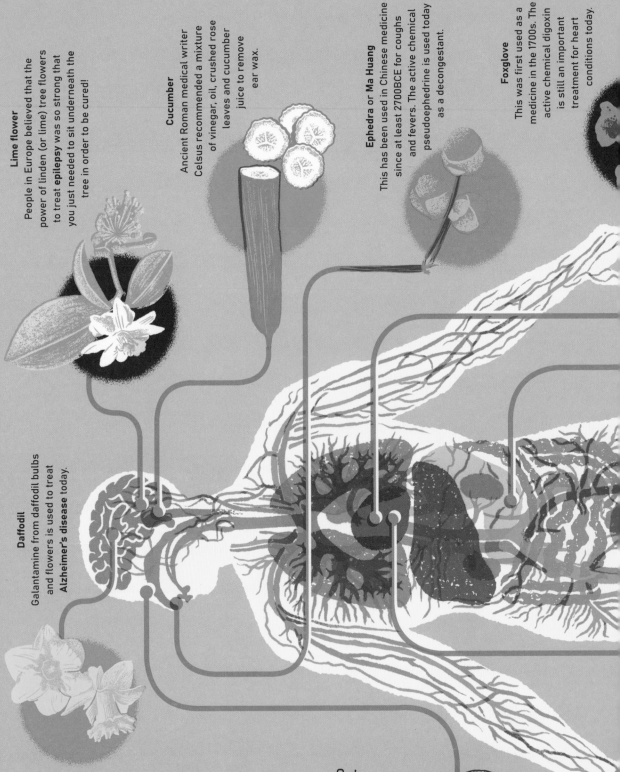

Belladonna

This is used in the Indian Ayurvedic tradition to treat asthma and chest complaints. Atropine, derived from the plant's active chemicals, is used to treat low heart rate today.

Senna

The leaves and seed pods of senna have been used as a **laxative** for thousands of years, and are still used today.

Lavender

This has been used for lots of medical complaints throughout history. In the 1600s in Europe, it was recommended by doctors to treat flatulence, or farting!

Madagascan periwinkle

Traditional healers in Madagascar used this plant to treat diabetes. In the 1950s, scientists discovered the active ingredients vinblastine and vincristine could be used to treat cancer.

Poppy

Since ancient times the thick juice from the capsule was used to treat pain, coughs and diarrhoea. It is still key to pain-relieving medicines today.

Crocus

Mentioned in the ancient Egyptian Ebers Papyrus (1550BCE) to treat swollen joints, the crocus has a long history as a treatment for **gout**. Its active ingredient, colchicine, is still used to treat gout today.

HERBALS AND PHYSIC GARDENS

From ancient times and increasingly after printing was invented, beautifully illustrated manuscripts and books known as 'herbals' shared botanical details and medical knowledge between countries and writers. In medieval Europe, monks and nuns created herb gardens to supply ingredients for medicines. In later centuries, those training to be a doctor or an apothecary, might have visited a physic garden to learn how to turn the plants into medicine.

CLOSE TO NATURE

People with beliefs closely linked to the natural world have always valued medicinal plants. Traditional medicine in New Zealand, known as rongoā Māori, is passed down through the generations, combining rongoā rākau (knowledge about native plants) with Te Oo Mai Reia (spiritual healing). Scientific innovation has meant that plant-based medicines have sometimes been either ignored or criticised. However, scientists continue to investigate plant chemicals to understand how they work and can inspire new medicines.

MALARIA MEDICINES

Malaria is one of the biggest killers in history. It is caused by a tiny parasite that lives in the blood and organs of its human or animal host and is spread by bloodsucking mosquitoes. Sufferers get a fever, chills, sweating, aches and pains, nausea and vomiting. Although we think of it as a tropical disease, it was also common in Europe, for example during the Roman Empire in Italy. Today, there are more than 200 million cases worldwide each year, with many thousands of deaths. Tragically, young children are at most risk of death, owing to a lack of immunity.

Early 1600s
Legendary cinchona

European travellers to South America discovered that bark from trees that grew in the cloud forests of the Andes mountains was an effective treatment for malaria. Legend has it that the life of the Countess of Chinchon, wife of the Viceroy of Peru, was miraculously saved when a local maid gave her medicine made from the bark. Her name – cinchona – was therefore given to the plant.

1820
Quinine is discovered

Exactly how cinchona worked was a mystery until its active ingredients, named cinchonine and quinine, were discovered by French chemists Joseph Bienaimé Caventou (1795–1877) and Pierre-Joseph Pelletier (1788–1842). Quinine, mainly in the form of pills or teas, was the main treatment for malaria until the mid-20th century.

1950s
Designing drugs

Pioneering American pharmacologists George Hitchings (1905–1998) and Gertrude Elion (1918–1999) developed pyrimethamine, specifically to treat malaria. They made a significant breakthrough, designing innovative medicines by creating new molecules that would interfere with the production of bacterial and viral DNA in cells (see page 25), and so stop infectious diseases from spreading.

1972
Amazing artemisinin

Inspired by Qing Hao, a traditional fever remedy based on Chinese wormwood, scientist Tu Youyou (born 1930) and her team successfully extracted the natural chemical artemisinin, which kills the malaria parasites at an early stage of their development. Drugs based on artemisinin have since reduced death rates dramatically. Tu Youyou was awarded the 2015 Nobel Prize in medicine for her discovery.

Late 1960s
Resistance proves problematic

Malaria cases increased owing to the parasite becoming resistant to existing treatments. American and Chinese scientists were under pressure to find new cures, particularly to keep their soldiers healthy during the Vietnam War.

1880
Parasite identified

Charles Louis Alphonse Laveran (1845–1922) first identified the malaria parasite. He was awarded the 1907 Nobel Prize in medicine for the discovery.

1898
Mosquitoes = malaria

Although mosquitoes have been found preserved in amber from up to 40 million years ago, the first scientists to establish fully their link with malaria were Ronald Ross (1857–1932) and Giovanni Battista Grassi (1854–1925). This discovery meant that people could now focus on preventing malaria. Ross won the 1902 Nobel Prize for this work.

1934
A false start

German scientist Johann 'Hans' Andersag (1902–55) created a very effective anti-malarial drug, inspired by quinine, but it was abandoned as it was too toxic for human use.

1943
Chloroquine put to use

American chemists redeveloped Andersag's drug, named it chloroquine, and put it into use, especially for soldiers fighting in tropical countries.

1990s
Masses of nets

Since the 1990s, mosquito nets treated with insecticide have been distributed in enormous quantities by international health organisations to protect people from being bitten, particularly while they are sleeping.

2021
Vaccine breakthrough

Following successful trials, the World Health Organisation announced that children in many African countries will be vaccinated against malaria. A successful vaccine that prevents people from catching malaria could be the key to controlling its impact worldwide.

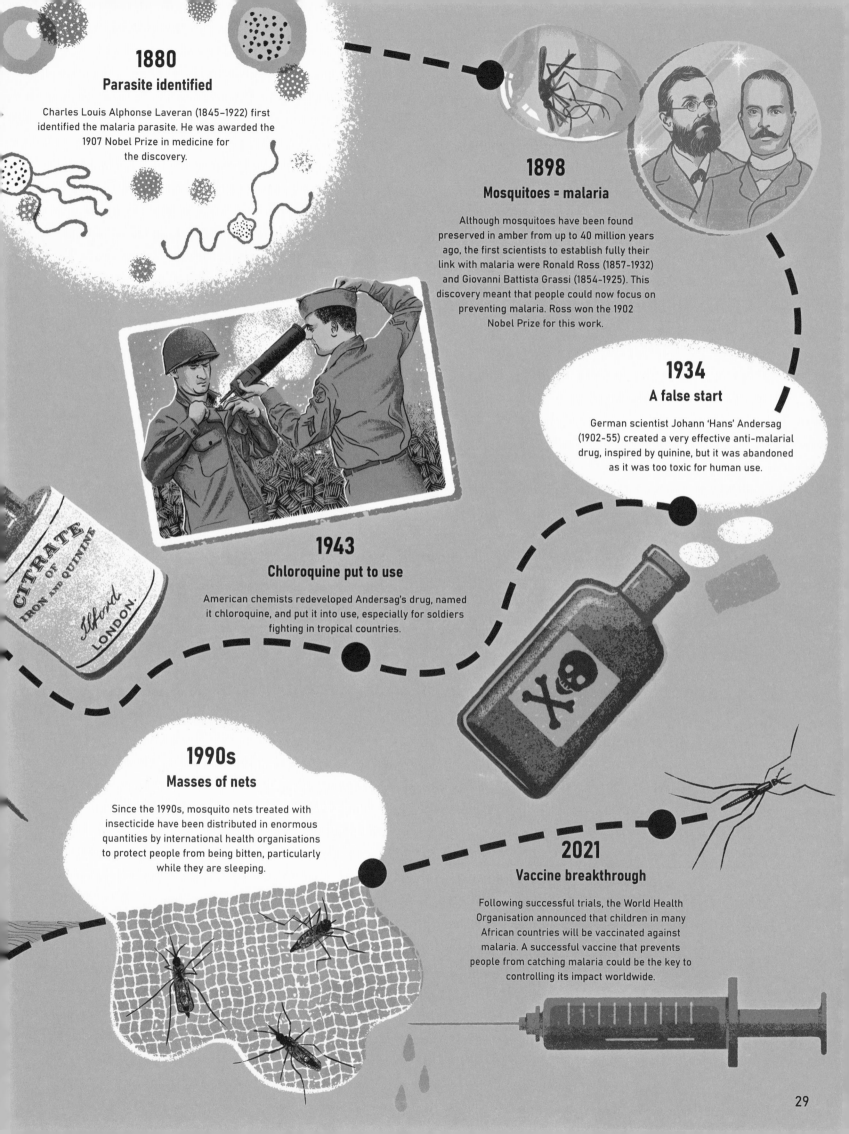

MAKING MEDICINES

How medicines are made has changed dramatically over time. If you opened your first aid kit today and found a cachet or a lohoch, you probably wouldn't have a clue what either was. These different types of medicine are now part of history, dating from a time when treatments were made individually by hand either at home or by an apothecary or pharmacist, often using techniques passed down the generations.

EXPERIMENTAL EQUIPMENT

As people experimented with more scientific ways to find medicinal ingredients, especially those from minerals and metals rather than plants, they developed equipment to help. Workshops to make drugs or investigate precious metals became full of intriguing devices.

During the 18th and 19th centuries, as more people earned wages and cities expanded, the demand for ready-made medicines grew. Apothecaries and **pharmacists** made pills, tinctures and syrups by hand in the back rooms of their shops (see page 32).

TAKING TABLETS

For every 10 medicines taken across the world today, an estimated 9 of them are tablets. The first tablets were made one by one in a little device invented by William Brockedon (1787–1854). The ingredients would be poured into the die and then punched with a mallet to compress all of the powders together. The next step was mass production. In the 1800s, the massive demand for medicines supported mass production. Henry Solomon Wellcome (1853–1936) and Silas Mainville Burroughs (1846–1895) established one of the biggest and earliest global medicine businesses.

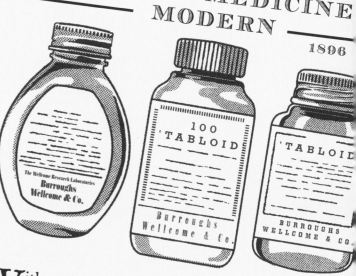

MAKING MEDICINE MODERN

1896

With this week's opening of the Wellcome Chemical Research Laboratories, pioneering American pharmaceutical entrepreneur Henry Solomon Wellcome continues to lead the way in medicines manufacture. Since he launched his company Burroughs Wellcome and Co in September 1880 with his late business partner Silas Mainville Burroughs, the business has gone from strength to strength. From their small manufactory in Wandsworth opened in 1883 to the impressive industrial complex in Dartford opened with a spectacular fete and firework display in 1889, what underpins this success is the desire to harness the latest science and manufacturing developments. The duo registered their innovative "compressed product" technology as Tabloids in 1883. Their dedicated local workforce, which has doubled over the last decade, the high calibre of their scientific staff, and their on-site farm for the production of medicinal plants such as deadly nightshade, foxglove and henbane means that their ability to reach a global market can only grow.

MAKING MILLIONS OF MEDICINES

Today, the journey of a drug from the laboratory to the patient takes around 12 years and costs around £1.15 billion. The research often starts in a university department with scientists exploring how a disease works and how it might be treated, funded by government or industry. New drugs might be based on animals, plants or fungi, but also on new molecules developed through scientists' growing knowledge of genetics and proteins. Thousands of potential compounds might be investigated before a handful are analysed more closely.

At this stage, the new medicine has to be tested on humans, starting with a very small group and building up to larger international studies. If a new medicine passes all of the many testing stages, the manufacturers will apply for permission to sell it. For every 25,000 substances that are developed in the laboratory, 25 are tested in humans, 5 make it to the patient and just 1 new medicine makes enough money to cover the cost of the whole process.

SELLING MEDICINES

How do you choose which medicine to buy? You might ask someone to recommend something that has worked for them, but you might also be persuaded by an advert. Adverts for medicines were once simply shouted in the market square or printed on a leaflet. Now they might be displayed on the side of a bus, shown on television or pop up on the internet. Cure-all promises used to be common, but now the claims that are made about a medicine's effectiveness are carefully controlled and must be as accurate as possible.

ROLL UP, ROLL UP!

Across Europe from around the 1600s, quack doctors with no formal qualifications travelled from town to town selling medicines to large crowds. The ingredients were at best useless, but with some medicines including mercury, opium, antimony and alcohol, they could also cause severe side effects or even death. Taking medicine was therefore a risky business!

A POWERFUL REMEDY!

CUSTOMISED CURES

In the 1700s, medicine sellers developed specially designed and shaped bottles to ensure their products were instantly recognisable. By the 1800s, every part of a medicine's packaging was carefully designed for maximum sales. Thomas Holloway (1800–83), who became a very rich man by selling pills and ointments, claimed that his ointment was sold by 'almost all respectable medicine vendors throughout the civilised world'. Medicine sellers used recommendations from satisfied customers, known as testimonials, to persuade other people to buy their products. We now know that many of these were made up by the advertiser.

SECRET FORMULAS

Until the late 1800s, most medicines were made by a pharmacist in their shop, either from their own recipes or for a doctor's prescription. Making up their own medicines was a good way for pharmacists to make a profit, and some became famous. Until new laws were passed in the 20th century, the ingredients in most medicines were kept a secret from the customer. Most people simply accepted that they had to place their trust in the knowledge of expert doctors and pharmacists.

Many adverts made the claim that medicines could cure diseases, even if this wasn't true. In the US and the UK, false advertising was outlawed in the 1930s and 1940s.

MARVELLOUS RESTORATIVE

THE BLOOD PURIFIER

CURES ALL ILLS

INTERNET SALES AND SCAMS

Although laws exist to protect us today, fraudulent medicines are still sold across the world. Fake brand-name treatments present a massive challenge and while the internet has meant it's easier to sell medicines safely, it's also made it easier to persuade people to buy dubious remedies.

POISONS

All medicines are poisons. The difference between them making you better or making you worse is the amount that you take. In the past, some doctors used metals like mercury and antimony to treat diseases including syphilis, typhoid and fevers, but many patients suffered just as much from the treatment as they did from the disease. Humans have learned how to use poisonous compounds to treat diseases, but they have also used them to get away with murder!

LEGENDARY PROTECTION

Legend has it that King Mithridates VI, who ruled Pontus, a kingdom in Asia Minor (now Turkey) between 120 and 63BCE, was so scared of being poisoned by his enemies that he invented an **antidote**, which he took daily. Viper flesh was a key ingredient as it was widely believed that snakes contained a substance that prevented them from poisoning themselves with their own venom. When the Romans conquered Pontus they seized the famed remedy, known as mithridatium. Emperor Nero (37–68CE) asked his physician, Andromachus, to improve on it, and the new recipe known as Theriaca Andromachi or Andromachus' treacle, together with the original mithridatium, dominated the market in poison antidotes for nearly two millennia.

CHEMOTHERAPY

Although safety is always key when using medicines, doctors still use poisonous substances to treat diseases like cancer. Chemotherapy drugs intentionally cause significant damage to cancer cells, but in the process lead to severe side effects including hair loss and nausea. Researchers continue to work on cancer treatments, that aim to target only the cancer cells with fewer side effects.

THE LAFARGE SCANDAL

In 1840, Frenchwoman Marie Lafarge (1816–52) was imprisoned for murdering her husband, Charles Pouch-Lafarge. The case hit the national headlines as the first to use a new scientific test – the Marsh Test, developed by Scottish chemist James Marsh in 1836 – to prove that she had poisoned him using arsenic.

PREVENTING POISONING

With many powerful substances available in apothecary shops and pharmacies by the 19th century, governments became concerned that the public was at risk. A spate of murders caused by poison led to new laws and regulations. In Victorian Britain, registered pharmacists had to pass exams in order to sell medicinal poisons such as strychnine and opium. The sales had to be to known customers and officially recorded, and the substances had to be safely stored in locked cupboards and in distinctive ribbed poison bottles to prevent any confusion.

HOSPITALS THROUGH HISTORY

Today, everybody expects to have access to a hospital, although in many countries receiving treatment is expensive. In the past, hospitals often played a role beyond providing medical treatment. Their remit today as a specialist centre for planned procedures and the expert care of emergency and long-term conditions has developed over time.

ANCIENT HEALING

Across Greece, ruins of ancient healing temples or asclepions can still be found, some dating from as early as 350BCE. People would visit to ask for help from gods (particularly Asclepius, the god of healing), and would receive medical treatment at the same time.

Archaeologists have found ancient Roman hospital buildings known as valetudinaria, especially in military forts, but it seems that wealthy people in towns were mainly treated in their own homes.

ISLAMIC HOSPITALS

Hospitals were built throughout Islamic lands, with some of the earliest ones founded in Baghdad, Iraq (805CE), and Cairo, Egypt (872CE). As well as treating the sick, they provided care for people recovering from illness or accidents and for those with mental health conditions, and also acted as a retirement home for those who didn't have family to look after them.

The largest hospital in Baghdad at this time was established in 982CE by ruler 'Adud al-Dawlah. In 1184, a traveller described it as being as large as an enormous palace. By the 12th century, Baghdad had 60 hospitals, whereas London had just one.

The reputation of Islamic hospitals grew in Europe and their influence spread, particularly after the wars between Christian and Muslim forces, known as the Crusades (1095-1291).

CHRISTIAN HOSPITALS

In Europe since the early 1100s, hospitals were Christian places, set up to help poor, homeless and sick people. The word 'hospital' comes from the hospitality that the religious orders offered, and people donated money to pay for their activities as part of their spiritual duty.

When King Henry VIII (1491-1547) dissolved the English and Welsh monasteries in the 1530s, religious hospitals closed too. Instead, local parishes and organisations looked after the poor and sick, and gradually hospitals were set up by volunteers and funded by local rich residents. Often these did not have the resources to treat people with long-term or infectious diseases, so specialist hospitals were created, particularly in cities. However, most sick people were still treated at home and going to hospital was a rare event.

TOWARDS TODAY'S HOSPITALS

During the 1800s, many more hospitals were built across the world, with their design reflecting a new understanding of the importance of cleanliness and the isolation of infectious patients. The number of doctors working in hospitals vastly increased as hands-on medical education grew. Developments in nursing, particularly through the work of Florence Nightingale (see page 64), also had an impact on staffing standards and aspects of hospital design such as the introduction of better ventilation, more windows and bigger wards.

The role of hospitals has increased dramatically in the past century. Significant developments in surgery (see pages 38-39), the introduction of scanning and monitoring (see pages 22-23), and different attitudes to childbirth (see pages 58-59) are just some of the factors that have increased hospitals' importance as key centres for healthcare.

EARLY SURGERY

Until recent history, surgery was only carried out in emergencies, so after accidents or life-threatening battle wounds. Patients remained wide awake and experienced agonising pain. Even if they survived an operation, they often died from infected wounds. And yet archaeologists have found skeletons of people who lived thousands of years ago who clearly survived amputation, complicated compound fractures and skull injuries.

Scalpel

Retractor

Hook for pulling out tissue

ANCIENT OPERATIONS

In ancient Rome, some of the earliest operations that historians know about were on wounded wrestlers, gladiators and soldiers. Archagathus emigrated from Greece to Italy in 219BCE and called himself vulnerarius or wound specialist. His recommendations included inserting a white-hot metal rod into the skin of a wrestler's armpit to prevent frequent dislocated arms. Roman surgeons used bone drills and skull-rasps to treat skull fractures, if perhaps someone had been kicked in the head by a horse. They would make the wound larger, lift the broken section of skull and then fill the hole with flour and boiling vinegar.

EXCRUCIATING CAUTERISATION

In the first century CE, Roman doctor Celsus provided details on how to stop wounds bleeding and advice about ulcers and **abscesses** in his encyclopaedia *De medicina*. One technique was cauterisation, where blood vessels or wounds were burnt using a hot metal instrument, to stop bleeding and close up the wound. It was hoped that it would stop infection, but it must have been excruciatingly painful. The technique was recommended for many centuries across Europe and the Middle East.

LEARNING FROM WAR WOUNDS

Once gunpowder was widely used in battles, the number and severity of war wounds increased massively, and doctors had to develop new techniques. In 1514, Italian surgeon Giovanni da Vigo (1450-1525) published a book in which he recommended treating bullet wounds with boiling oil. French surgeon Ambroise Paré (1510-90) was a pioneer in treating battlefield wounds, and in 1545 he published a book specifically about wounds caused by firearms. One day, he ran out of boiling oil and instead used egg yolk, rose oil and turpentine on a wound. When he returned the next morning, he was astonished to find that the wound was healing successfully. He claimed that he would never use oil again as it was cruel and painful.

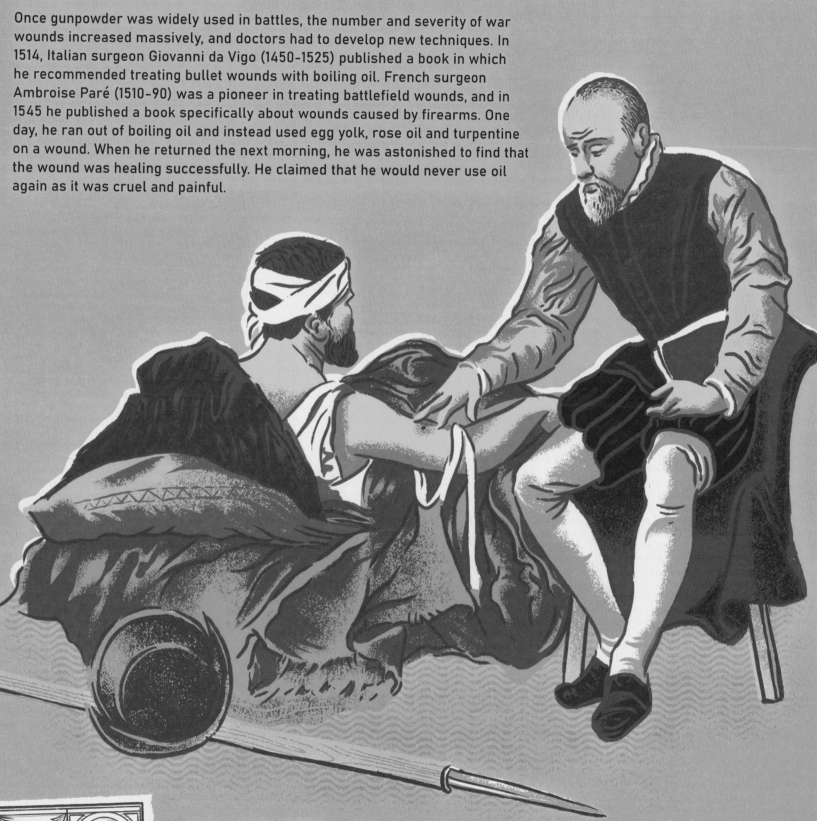

REBUILDING FACES

In Italy in the 1580s, Gaspare Tagliacozzi (1545-99) was professor of surgery and anatomy at the University of Bologna. He became renowned for carrying out reconstructions of the nose and other missing parts of patients' faces which had been injured owing to war, duels or disease. These techniques had long been practised in India and described by doctors including Sushruta (6th century BCE). In his illustrated book called *De curtorum chirurgia per insitionem* (On the Surgical Restoration of Defects), first published in 1597, he wrote that his aim was to help the spirit and the mind of the injured person rather than to produce a result that delighted the eye. Much later, surgeons trying to treat the terrible facial injuries of soldiers in the First World War were inspired by these earlier attempts.

THE WONDER OF ANAESTHESIA

Surgery without pain relief was, as you can imagine, excruciatingly painful. Alcohol, opium and cannabis have all been used since ancient times to reduce a patient's pain, but the development of anaesthesia truly revolutionised surgery. From a Japanese herbal concoction to propofol, today's drug of choice, the race to find the most effective general anaesthetic has seen pioneering scientists, doctors and dentists compete and inspire each other.

HANAOKA SEISHŪ – THE POWER OF PLANTS

Medical history often focuses on European developments, but Japanese surgeon Hanaoka Seishū (1760–1835) was probably the first to use a general anaesthetic. Inspired by ancient Chinese medicines, he developed tsusensan – a mixture of powerful plants. Its effects lasted for up to 24 hours and allowed Hanaoka to experiment on his wife. Patients arrived from all over Japan, and Hanaoka performed plastic surgeries, **amputations** and more than 150 breast cancer operations. However, his expertise did not spread beyond Japan, and so his achievements had no impact in America or Europe, where similar surgical techniques were not used for another 40 years.

JOSEPH PRIESTLEY – LAUGHING GAS

Having discovered oxygen in 1771, British chemist Joseph Priestley (1733-1804) discovered nitrous oxide the following year. Pioneering scientist Humphrey Davy (1778-1829) named it 'laughing gas' because of the euphoria it caused, but having used it to numb the pain from his own wisdom teeth he suggested using it in surgery. Instead, it was mainly used for fun – at parties and for entertainment!

In December 1844, American dentist Horace Wells (1815-48) observed that participants in a demonstration of the use of laughing gas didn't notice when they injured themselves. He arranged a public demonstration at Harvard Medical School, but the patient cried out in pain and a disillusioned Wells gave up. Today, it is used by mothers in labour, and to relax and reduce pain for injured patients.

ROBERT LISTON – ETHER

In 1730, German chemist August Sigmund Frobenius (1700-41) gave the name 'ether' to a highly **flammable** substance. Although Paracelsus (1493-1541) had used it to send chickens to sleep 200 years earlier, it was American surgeons and dentists who introduced it to medicine.

In 1842, Dr Crawford Williamson Long (1815-78) was probably the first to use ether for surgery. But the demonstration that made headlines was the removal of a tumour by Dr John Warren (1753-1815) on 16 October 1846. Dentist William Morton also successfully numbed his patients' pain. The news spread quickly, and the first two British anaesthetics were likely given on the same day, 19 December 1846. Surgeon Robert Liston (1794-1847) amputated a patient's leg using ether just two days later, its first public demonstration in Europe.

Ether was easier to use than nitrous oxide, which had to be produced using complicated equipment in the operating theatre.

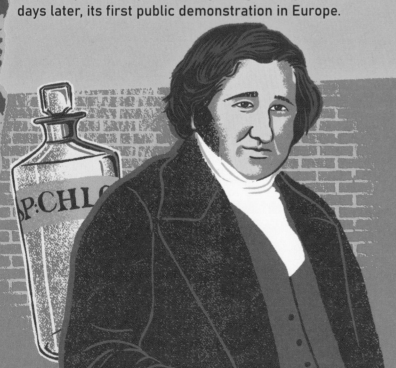

JAMES YOUNG SIMPSON – CHLOROFORM

In 1847, Liston's student James Young Simpson (1811-1870) first demonstrated the anaesthetic qualities of chloroform by testing it on himself and his two assistants. It was safer than ether, which was highly flammable and irritated the patient's nose, lungs and throat, but both substances continued to be used through the 1800s. When Queen Victoria asked John Snow (see page 50) to give her chloroform for the birth of Prince Leopold in 1853 and Princess Beatrice in 1857, its popularity increased.

ANTISEPSIS

Even if surgery is successful, it is vital that a patient's wounds heal successfully too. Ancient treatments included frankincense and turpentine, and surgeons cauterised wounds to stop bleeding, but there was no scientific understanding of what was causing infection until the late 1800s.

HAND WASHING

Hungarian physician Ignaz Semmelweiss (1818–1865) was worried about how many new mothers were dying from infections after childbirth at Vienna General Hospital in the 1840s. He started to collect data and found that women who were looked after by medical students were more likely to die than those who were attended by a midwife. What was happening? As was usual at the time, the students were examining dead bodies as well as helping mothers, and were spreading infection. Semmelweiss introduced hand washing with a chlorine solution, and death rates quickly fell.

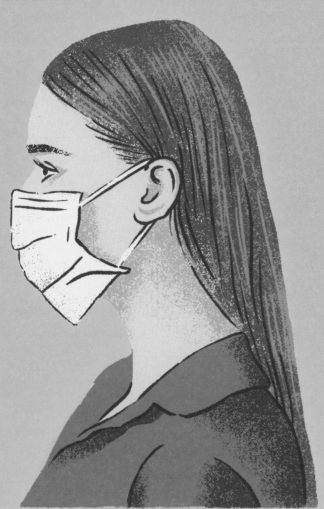

GERM THEORY AND ASEPTIC SURGERY

Until the late 1800s, surgeons didn't keep themselves, their instruments or the operating theatre clean. They often wore coats or aprons covered in blood from previous operations, as evidence of their experience, and if they washed their hands it was after an operation, but not before. Medical students were also allowed to watch operations close up. Interest in Pasteur and Koch's new germ theory (see page 15) coupled with a growing number of industrial injuries such as complex fractures inspired surgeons to rethink their techniques.

By the late 1800s, **aseptic** surgery was introduced, which aimed to stop germs getting into the operating theatre and therefore into a patient's wound. Surgeons began to wear gloves, face masks and clean gowns, replaced wooden operating tables with metal ones that could be more easily cleaned, and used sterilised surgical instruments. These practices continue today.

Surgeon Joseph Lister (1827–1912) was inspired by Pasteur's breakthroughs in understanding germs. While working in Glasgow in the 1860s, he developed a device that sprayed carbolic acid solution across the patient, staff and operating area. Lister also covered wounds with carbolic-soaked dressings, starting with 11-year-old James Greenless who had badly broken his leg in August 1865. Rather than becoming infected and having to be amputated, James's leg got better. Lister wrote about his success in *The Lancet* medical journal. He also experimented with hand washing and sterilising instruments, a practice that became known as **antisepsis**. Not everyone agreed with Lister's approach, either because they didn't believe in germ theory or because they thought that carbolic acid could make wounds worse. But Lister's results showed great success. More people survived their operations, and as a result, surgeons could consider procedures that were once unthinkable.

PUBLIC HEALTH

Keeping healthy is not just about what you do as an individual. We live in households, towns, cities and countries and can even regard ourselves as global citizens. The way that we live alongside each other, and the measures that governments and other organisations take to keep us healthy, have an impact on us all.

HYGIENE

In the ancient world, the rulers of enormous cities like Rome and Alexandria invested in public water supplies, drains, public baths and toilets to keep the population clean and healthy.

Hygiene and cleanliness were also very important in the ancient Muslim world, partly linked to ritual washing (wudhu) before the five daily prayers. Although Roman public baths were largely abandoned in western Europe, they remained in Islamic countries.

SUPPORT THE MATCHGIRLS' STRIKE

STRIKE!

WE SHALL BE HEARD!

NO MORE PHOSSY JAW!

CONTAMINATION IN THE CITY

As cities across the world grew bigger, the challenges increased. London, the largest city in the world in the 1800s, simply did not have the systems to cope with so much human waste. Many households shared the same outdoor toilet, which emptied into the road or the local river, polluting water people also used for bathing and drinking. Putrid matter even leaked out of overcrowded graveyards. With families crowded together, infectious diseases spread easily and caused many deaths.

There was an increase in available jobs in factories, coal mines and docks. Young children worked long hours in risky environments alongside their families, until a series of laws were passed from the 1840s. In 1888, around 1,500 girls employed to make matches in the East End of London went on strike to protest about their terrible working conditions, in particular a horrible disease nicknamed 'phossy jaw' which they got from working with toxic white phosphorous.

GLOBAL HEALTH

In Great Britain, the National Health Service was established in 1948, just after the Second World War ended. It was the first time anywhere in the world that all visits to the dentist, doctor and hospital were free of charge.

Also in 1948, the World Health Organisation was set up to enable a global approach to health, particularly instigating major projects like vaccination and safer childbirth, and tackling challenging diseases such as smallpox and malaria (see pages 28–29). Today, it continues to offer advice and encourage countries to work together.

PLAGUES AND PANDEMICS

Diseases can spread so fast and so far that they become out of control. When the spread becomes global, it is described as a pandemic. From ancient empires to the present day, enormous numbers of people have suffered from infectious diseases including the plague, cholera (pages 50-51), AIDS and SARS. Today, we have medicines to prevent or treat most of these infections, but the recent COVID-19 pandemic shows that diseases can still present enormous challenges.

ANCIENT PLAGUES

Between the 5th century BCE and the 6th century CE, a number of devastating disease outbreaks killed millions of people from Greece to China, and across the Roman Empire. Although historians believe that the **pandemics** were caused by diseases including the bubonic plague and smallpox, no one knows for sure what the deadly infections were.

BUBONIC PLAGUE

Plague is a potentially lethal infectious disease, caused by a bacterium called *Yersinia pestis*. This bacterium lives in some animals (mainly rats and mice) and fleas. Bubonic plague is the most common form of the disease. In 1346, the Black Death killed up to 200 million people across Asia, the Middle East, North Africa and Europe (more on pages 48-49). In 1665, an estimated 100,000 Londoners died in the Great Plague of London – the worst outbreak of bubonic plague in England since the Black Death. In 1855, the plague spread easily from China via global shipping routes to every inhabited continent on Earth, in a pandemic that lasted until the 1960s.

SMALLPOX AND MEASLES

As European people colonised countries in Africa and the Americas from the 1400s, they introduced devastating new diseases. Imported viruses, including smallpox, killed an estimated 90% of native people living in North, South and Central America, while **measles** killed more than half the populations of Cuba and Honduras in the 1500s.

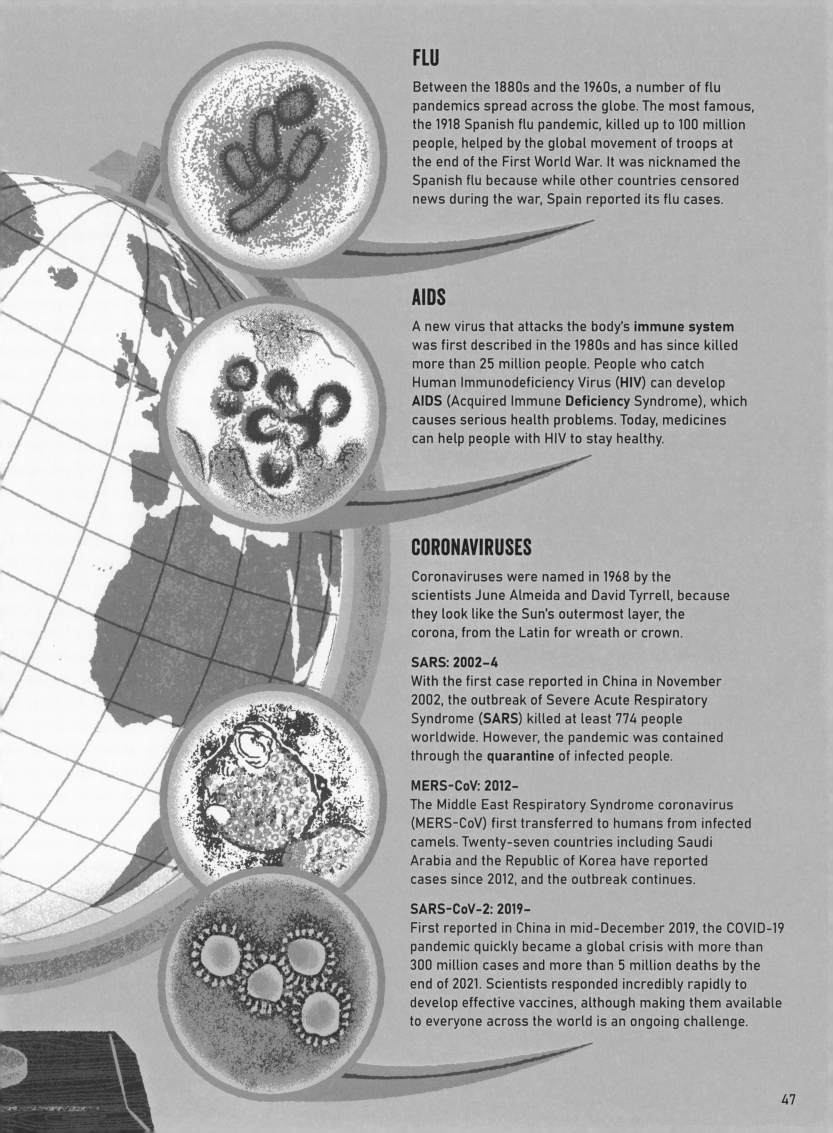

FLU

Between the 1880s and the 1960s, a number of flu pandemics spread across the globe. The most famous, the 1918 Spanish flu pandemic, killed up to 100 million people, helped by the global movement of troops at the end of the First World War. It was nicknamed the Spanish flu because while other countries censored news during the war, Spain reported its flu cases.

AIDS

A new virus that attacks the body's **immune system** was first described in the 1980s and has since killed more than 25 million people. People who catch Human Immunodeficiency Virus (**HIV**) can develop **AIDS** (Acquired Immune **Deficiency** Syndrome), which causes serious health problems. Today, medicines can help people with HIV to stay healthy.

CORONAVIRUSES

Coronaviruses were named in 1968 by the scientists June Almeida and David Tyrrell, because they look like the Sun's outermost layer, the corona, from the Latin for wreath or crown.

SARS: 2002–4
With the first case reported in China in November 2002, the outbreak of Severe Acute Respiratory Syndrome (**SARS**) killed at least 774 people worldwide. However, the pandemic was contained through the **quarantine** of infected people.

MERS-CoV: 2012–
The Middle East Respiratory Syndrome coronavirus (MERS-CoV) first transferred to humans from infected camels. Twenty-seven countries including Saudi Arabia and the Republic of Korea have reported cases since 2012, and the outbreak continues.

SARS-CoV-2: 2019–
First reported in China in mid-December 2019, the COVID-19 pandemic quickly became a global crisis with more than 300 million cases and more than 5 million deaths by the end of 2021. Scientists responded incredibly rapidly to develop effective vaccines, although making them available to everyone across the world is an ongoing challenge.

THE BLACK DEATH

In the 14th century, a terrifying disease killed up to 200 million people across Asia, the Middle East, North Africa and Europe. This massive outbreak of bubonic plague was the deadliest pandemic in recorded history. At the time, no one knew what caused or spread the disease and there was no cure. Today, there are still regular outbreaks of plague in places like Madagascar, but it can now be successfully treated with antibiotics.

ATTACK OF THE PLAGUE

The bubonic plague is an ancient disease thought to have begun in the 1200s in the area that is now Uzbekistan and Kyrgyzstan. Historians and scientists believe that infected fleas living on wild marmots carried a specific bacterium in their blood, which transferred the plague to humans with a bite. Most people lived in crowded dirty conditions, and so the infection travelled easily via fleas on rats, and via lice living on unwashed clothing and bedlinen. The disease spread as merchants travelled to Constantinople and on across Europe, the Middle East and North Africa. The pestilence, as it was known at the time, was particularly bad in England and in modern-day Italy and Germany. The pandemic peaked between 1347 and 1351, but there continued to be many plague outbreaks centuries after this.

ACHES, PAINS, LUMPS AND BUMPS

The plague was an extremely frightening illness. You might have begun to feel hot, achy and tired before starting to develop buboes, or swollen infected lymph nodes, in your groin, neck and armpits. Very few people recovered; some died within 24 hours, but most within one week.

PREVENTION AND QUARANTINE

Many people believed that the plague was a punishment sent by God, so they visited churches and prayed in an attempt to protect themselves. Some doctors believed that the disease might have been caused by poisonous gases or miasmas which could spread easily from a sick to a healthy person. A pomander filled with scented herbs was thought to help to block out the disease.

Doctors such as Guy de Chauliac (1300-1368) from France and Ibn al-Khatib (1313-74) from Spain, who lived through the pandemic, highlighted ways to prevent the disease which we champion today, for example the importance of having fresh air, cleaning rooms and staying away from infected people. In a number of ports, people arriving on ships were ordered to stay offshore for 40 days – this is where our word quarantine originates, coming from the Italian word for the number 40.

Today, we recognise the doctor with a beaked mask as a symbol of the plague. In fact, this type of doctor's outfit wasn't worn until the 1600s.

LOOKING BACK

In 1894, French-Swiss doctor Alexandre Yersin (1863-1943) discovered the *Yersinia pestis* bacterium. Today, scientists can analyse the DNA of skeletons of people who died during the 14th-century pandemic, to look for fragments of the *Yersinia pestis* bacterium.

49

CHOLERA

On 18 October 1831, 12-year-old Isabella Hazard from Sunderland was one of the first people to die of cholera in Britain. She had fallen ill very suddenly, experiencing severe vomiting and diarrhoea and an unquenchable thirst. Her eyes sunk into their sockets and her skin turned worryingly blue. The fact that four major cholera epidemics in Britain in the 1800s caused more than 140,000 deaths signalled that something was clearly very wrong. Subsequent investigations played a significant role in highlighting the link between living conditions, public health and infectious diseases.

ORIGINS AND SPREAD

Cholera's arrival in Sunderland was part of a global pandemic that originated in the Bengal region of eastern India. In the mid-1800s, as British colonisers expanded their influence across India, new railways and canals meant that the British Army spread the disease. Increased movement of people around the world, including on British trade ships during this time of empire-building, meant that millions died as cholera reached Asia, the Middle East, Europe, East Africa and North America. Those infected often died within 24 hours as there was no cure.

CAUSES

For decades, scientists, doctors and government officials investigated different causes for the disease. Many believed miasmas (see page 15) were to blame, but in the 1850s, the doctor John Snow (1813–58) argued that cholera was spread through dirty water, famously linking the supply of water from a pump in Soho, London, to an outbreak in the neighbourhood. While Snow correctly identified cholera as a waterborne disease, it wasn't until 1884 that Robert Koch discovered the actual bacteria that caused it.

CONTROLLING THE DISEASE

Although we now know that diseases are not spread by foul-smelling air or mist, taking actions to prevent miasmas led to better hygiene and living conditions, and ultimately helped control disease. Englishman Edwin Chadwick (1800-90) carried out a report for government in 1842. He concluded that urban poverty, disease, dirt and miasmas were all linked, and that if you cleaned up the city, you would simultaneously reduce disease and improve people's lives.

The government understood that investing in better **sewage** and drainage systems, water supplies and housing meant that the economy stayed strong too. They passed laws to implement changes across the country, starting with a Public Health Act in 1848. But it took many decades to take effect. In 1858 in London, the river Thames, full of human and animal sewage and industrial pollution, smelt so terrible that it was called the Great Stink.

CHOLERA TODAY

The world is still experiencing a cholera epidemic: it started in South Asia in 1961, reaching Africa in 1971 and then the Americas in 1991. Cholera is now **endemic** in many countries, with an estimated four million cases each year across the world, and up to 140,000 deaths. Today, cholera is easily treated if caught early, and the development of cholera vaccines from the 1980s onwards has had a significant impact. The World Health Organisation is co-ordinating efforts to eliminate cholera in 20 of the hardest hit countries by 2030.

VACCINATION

What if you could stop an infectious disease before it even starts? Today, vaccination means that once life-threatening illnesses, such as polio, measles and mumps, are rare. By giving people a very small harmless form of a disease, vaccines teach the immune system to produce the right antibodies to attack it. If most people are vaccinated, the disease can't spread.

SMALLPOX

Smallpox is a terrifying incurable disease which starts with a fever and develops to cover your whole body in a blistering rash which can be fatal or cause blindness and terrible scarring if you are lucky enough to survive. Most victims have been children under five years old. Scientists believe that it originally came from Asian gerbils, with the earliest written descriptions from ancient India and China. Scars on the mummified body of ancient Egyptian Pharaoh Ramses V suggest that his death in 1145BCE was caused by smallpox; 16-year-old King Edward VI died of it in 1553; and it killed an estimated 300 million people globally in the 20th century.

INOCULATION

For centuries, people in countries as far apart as Wales, India and Turkey noticed that if you had already had smallpox, you were protected from getting it again or spreading it to others. They used a technique known as inoculation to infect people deliberately. Dried smallpox scabs were rubbed into – or infected pus was transferred to – a cut in a healthy person. In the early 1700s in America, enslaved African people introduced smallpox inoculation to their European owners.
In 1721, Lady Mary Wortley Montagu (1689–1762) introduced the practice to Europe. She had witnessed the power of inoculation first-hand while her husband was British ambassador in Constantinople. Having had her son inoculated in Turkey, on her return to London she invited influential doctors to watch the unfamiliar procedure being performed on her daughter. Although she faced strong opposition, her upper-class connections meant that confidence began to spread. After her death her letters from Turkey championing inoculation were published, and her pioneering work was given the credit it deserves.

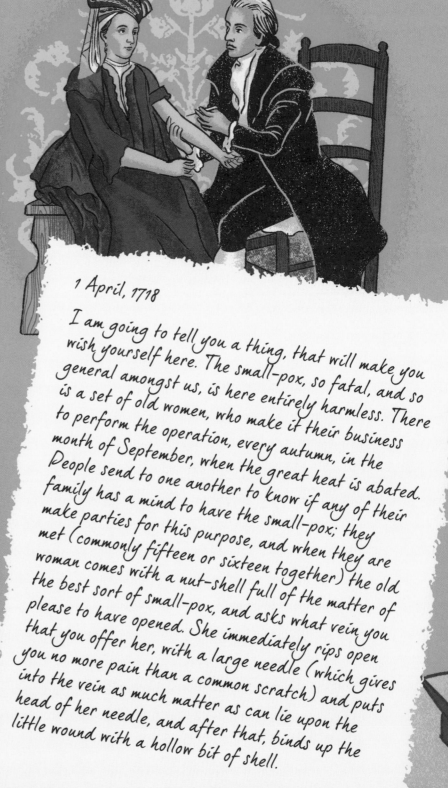

1 April, 1718

I am going to tell you a thing, that will make you wish yourself here. The small-pox, so fatal, and so general amongst us, is here entirely harmless. There is a set of old women, who make it their business to perform the operation, every autumn, in the month of September, when the great heat is abated. People send to one another to know if any of their family has a mind to have the small-pox; they make parties for this purpose, and when they are met (commonly fifteen or sixteen together) the old woman comes with a nut-shell full of the matter of the best sort of small-pox, and asks what vein you please to have opened. She immediately rips open that you offer her, with a large needle (which gives you no more pain than a common scratch) and puts into the vein as much matter as can lie upon the head of her needle, and after that, binds up the little wound with a hollow bit of shell.

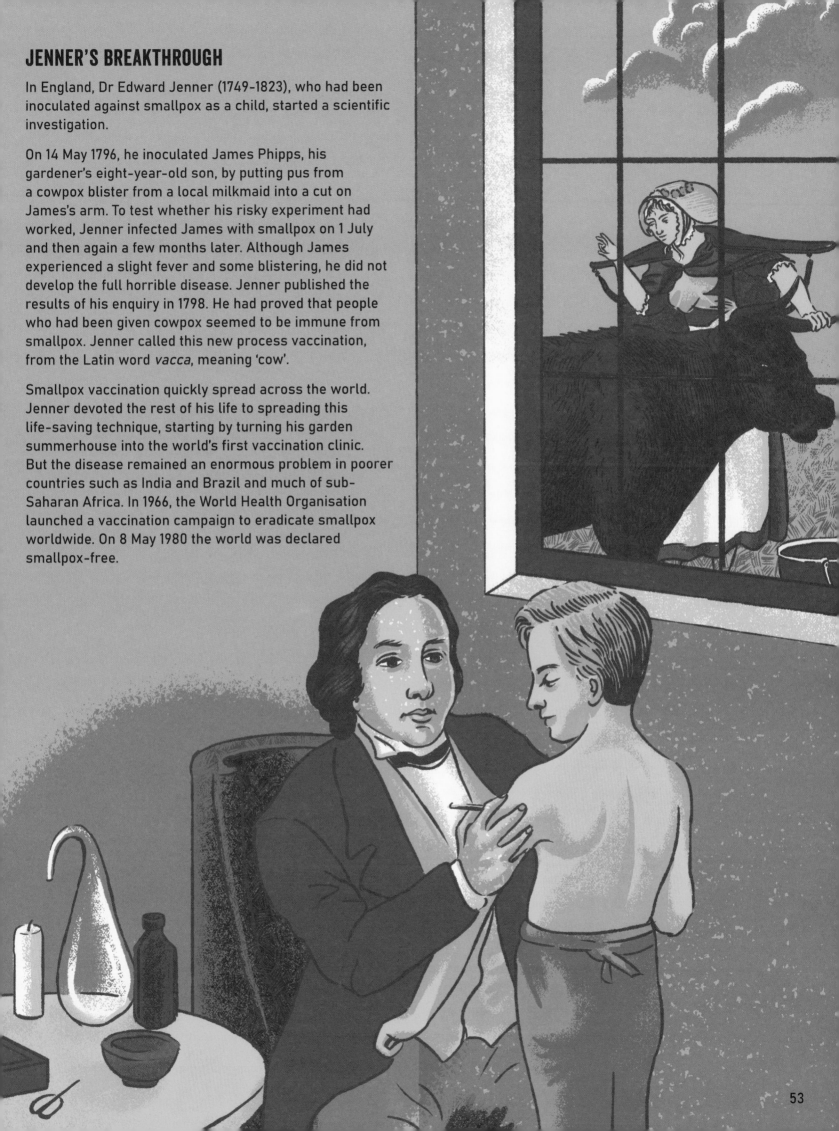

JENNER'S BREAKTHROUGH

In England, Dr Edward Jenner (1749–1823), who had been inoculated against smallpox as a child, started a scientific investigation.

On 14 May 1796, he inoculated James Phipps, his gardener's eight-year-old son, by putting pus from a cowpox blister from a local milkmaid into a cut on James's arm. To test whether his risky experiment had worked, Jenner infected James with smallpox on 1 July and then again a few months later. Although James experienced a slight fever and some blistering, he did not develop the full horrible disease. Jenner published the results of his enquiry in 1798. He had proved that people who had been given cowpox seemed to be immune from smallpox. Jenner called this new process vaccination, from the Latin word *vacca*, meaning 'cow'.

Smallpox vaccination quickly spread across the world. Jenner devoted the rest of his life to spreading this life-saving technique, starting by turning his garden summerhouse into the world's first vaccination clinic. But the disease remained an enormous problem in poorer countries such as India and Brazil and much of sub-Saharan Africa. In 1966, the World Health Organisation launched a vaccination campaign to eradicate smallpox worldwide. On 8 May 1980 the world was declared smallpox-free.

ONGOING CHALLENGES

Although vaccination has made a massive difference to world health, viruses are still very tricky diseases to treat and prevent. There is also a long history of people being wary about receiving vaccines, and this continues today.

OPPOSITION

In Britain in the 1720s, smallpox inoculation was initially carried out on powerless prisoners and orphaned children; they all survived and the prisoners were set free in thanks. By the 19th century, the clear success of smallpox vaccination meant governments wanted all children to be treated. In 1853, smallpox vaccination was made compulsory for all babies in England. Parents who refused to vaccinate their children were fined, or even put in prison. But some people believed that smallpox vaccines caused madness, diabetes or even death. Others feared that putting material from cows into humans might cause cancer or displease God. The government decided that, although vaccination was undoubtedly effective, parents could opt out. However, compulsory vaccination for smallpox continued in the UK until 1948.

Persuading people that vaccines are safe and will make a real difference to everyone's health is an ongoing challenge, most recently seen in the case of the global COVID-19 pandemic.

In 1885, around 100,000 protesters against vaccination marched through Leicester with banners, and burnt an effigy of Edward Jenner.

DOWN WITH COMPULSORY VACCINATION

MOVING TARGETS

Although scientists today are experts in creating vaccines to treat specific diseases, the viruses themselves alter over time and so the vaccines need to adapt, too. These variants can be difficult to predict. Researchers developed the first flu vaccine, used on British troops in the 1930s, from the virus itself. This meant that it was only effective against that specific virus. Scientists are still working today to develop a universal flu vaccine which would work against all variants of the disease.

THE COMMON COLD

Probably the most famous incurable virus is the common cold. Colds are caused by a number of viruses including members of the coronavirus family, first identified by June Almeida (1930–2007) in 1965 using a substance that came out of the snotty nose of an English schoolchild.

The Common Cold Unit, based in a former military hospital near Salisbury, was set up in 1946 to investigate the cause of the common cold. At least 18,000 volunteers stayed there over a period of 30 years, giving doctors a chance to identify around 200 cold viruses and to test drugs that might treat them.

BECOMING A DOCTOR: THE FIGHT FOR EQUALITY

Having a specialist person in the community who was expert in treating diseases or caring for the sick has been common since ancient times. Although this has always included women, their work has typically been unpaid – caring for their families and communities. In the past, most healers (men and women) learned from experienced practitioners, rather than taking exams. Today, doctors are nationally registered to ensure that they have the highest standards of knowledge, but when stricter medical qualifications were introduced, women struggled to jump the required hurdles.

STRICT CONTROL

In Britain, the first medical school opened at Oxford University in the 1300s. The College of Physicians was founded in London in 1518, to control the standards of people practising medicine. But women were strictly forbidden. Medical organisations intentionally excluded 'quack doctors' (see page 32), but their entrance requirements also shut out men who could not afford to go to university, and all women, as they were not allowed to sit the required exams. This was formalised further when a series of laws relating to registering for the British medical profession were passed from the 1850s.

Although the call for men to fight abroad allowed women to take up new medical opportunities (as well as opportunities in many other professions) during the First and Second World Wars, it wasn't until the 1970s that medical schools accepted women and men equally in many countries. Today in Britain, although there are more women than men working as general practitioners, for example, gender stereotypes and practical issues around family-friendly working still present challenges.

GLIMPSING MEDICAL WOMEN

Finding information about women who had medical roles is often challenging because there is little surviving evidence. However, an ancient Egyptian tomb from around 2700BCE names a woman called Merit Ptah who is described as the Chief Physician. Surviving Italian medical writings from the 1100s were probably written by Trota, a woman, and other books refer to women connected to the medical school at Salerno, Italy. Founded in the ninth century CE, the school was probably the first in world, and unusually it accepted both men and women as students and teachers.

FEMALE PIONEERS

Women had to overcome significant hurdles to qualify formally as doctors, facing prejudice from both men and women about their abilities. Some people believed that women were too weak, squeamish and unreliable to be trusted with patients. Others argued that it was vital for women to work in medicine, so that female patients felt confident about getting advice and treatment. Individual women worked hard to battle for their place in the profession, often against strong opposition.

DOROTHEA ERXLEBEN (1715-1762)

THE FIRST WOMAN TO GET A MEDICAL DEGREE

Determined to study medicine alongside her brother, Erxleben managed to get permission from Fredrick II of Prussia to study at the University of Halle in 1741. For reasons unknown, neither sibling took up the place. However, after years of successfully being a clergy wife with nine children as well as running her father's medical practice, Erxleben finally graduated from Halle in 1754. She practised medicine until her death, but no other woman was admitted to any German medical school until the 20th century.

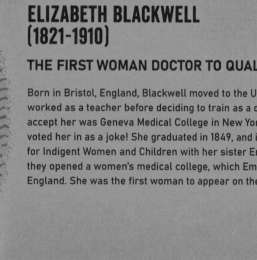

ELIZABETH BLACKWELL (1821-1910)

THE FIRST WOMAN DOCTOR TO QUALIFY IN THE UNITED STATES

Born in Bristol, England, Blackwell moved to the US with her family as a child and worked as a teacher before deciding to train as a doctor. The only medical college to accept her was Geneva Medical College in New York State. The all-male student body voted her in as a joke! She graduated in 1849, and in 1857 opened the New York Infirmary for Indigent Women and Children with her sister Emily, also a doctor. A decade later they opened a women's medical college, which Emily ran while Elizabeth moved back to England. She was the first woman to appear on the new Medical Register in 1859.

ELIZABETH GARRETT ANDERSON (1836-1917)

THE FIRST WOMAN TO QUALIFY AS A DOCTOR IN BRITAIN

As British medical schools did not accept women, Garrett Anderson combined private lessons and hospital work to qualify. The Society of Apothecaries was the only place that let her take their exams in 1865 – they then excluded women for a further 23 years! Garrett Anderson opened St Mary's Dispensary for Women and Children in 1866. In 1883, she was appointed dean of the London School of Medicine for Women, the first school where women could train to be doctors in Britain. She was also an active member of the suffrage movement, campaigning for women's equal rights, and the first woman mayor in England, elected in 1908.

MIDWIFERY

Although childbirth is a natural process, it can also prove dangerous for both mothers and babies. For centuries, midwives have assisted birthing mothers, traditionally as unpaid women working in their communities. Historically, men were not allowed into the delivery room, whether they were fathers or doctors – and certainly not as midwives themselves.

SHARING EXPERTISE

Midwives traditionally learnt their role from other experienced women, but from the 1500s they might have also consulted guidance books, if they were able to read. In 1609, Louise Bourgeois (1563–1636), midwife to the French queen Marie de Medici, wrote a book recording her observations of more than 2,000 births.

THE INVENTION OF FORCEPS

In 1813, a box of specialist surgical instruments was discovered under the floorboards in the Chamberlen family home in Essex, UK. Four generations of Chamberlens were male midwives, with Peter (1560-1631) serving Anne of Denmark, wife of King James I, and Henrietta Maria, wife of King Charles I. The hidden box included four pairs of forceps – curved metal tongs that fit round a baby's head and help with a difficult delivery. They were probably invented by the family, to give them a significant advantage over other midwives in helping with successful births. When they tried and failed to obtain a patent for their forceps they instead kept them secret. Rumour has it that they drove to births in closed or curtained carriages, with the birthing mother blindfolded and the forceps in an enormous, gold-covered box that required at least two people to carry it!

BATTLE OF THE SEXES

From the 1700s, so-called 'man-midwives' (early **obstetricians**) felt that births should involve doctors and instruments. They argued that their medical expertise was vital, but most female midwives maintained that birth should be natural, and that women should take the lead. Many also felt it was inappropriate for men to assist with childbirth.

Scottish-born William Smellie (1697-1763), known as the 'father of British midwifery', observed and published details of the natural birthing process and taught midwives and medical students through attending actual births.

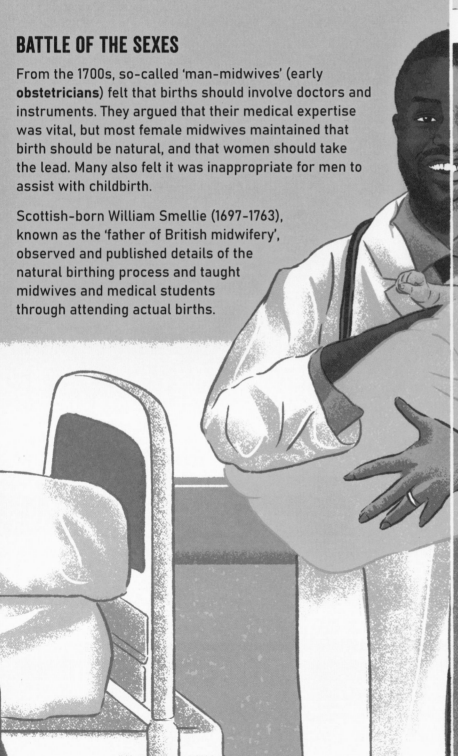

Midwives still experience a battle of the sexes in the 21st century, but this time it's being fought by men. The British 1951 Midwives Act even banned men from working as midwives altogether, and male midwives were not allowed in many countries into the late 20th century. Although this is no longer the case, less than 1% of midwives today are male.

BECOMING A SPECIALIST: DENTISTRY

Although the job of a dentist was only given a specific name in the 1700s, finding someone to pull out a rotten tooth or recommend a cure for toothache has always been important. Even though the advice given, the products used and the people involved back then might seem very strange to our modern eyes (and teeth!), getting rid of terrible tooth pain meant that dentistry emerged as an essential specialist job. In the later 20th century, public health campaigns about keeping your teeth clean and avoiding sugary foods have tried to prevent the need for dental work.

BARBER SURGEONS AND TOOTH DRAWERS

Early dentistry was mainly about stopping pain rather than preventing the cause, which meant the job basically fell to those who had the sharpest tools! In medieval Europe you could go to blacksmiths, wigmakers, jewellers or apothecaries to have your teeth pulled out. Barber surgeons were the most common choice, however, as they were experienced in dental procedures as well as cutting hair. Specialist tooth drawers also travelled around the country taking out teeth at markets and fairs. While some were con artists who did nothing but put on a show, some came highly recommended. King Henry IV (1367–1413) even had his own personal tooth drawer. From the early 1700s, dental keys were used to extract teeth, but they gripped so tightly that gum and bone often came out along with the tooth, and sometimes patients even ended up with a broken jaw!

TIME TO GET PROFESSIONAL

As dentistry become more specialised, most practitioners learnt the ropes through an apprenticeship, but they were not expected to have a degree or pass any exams. In London, the first dental hospitals opened in the 1850s with teaching schools attached. It wasn't until 1878, however, that a law was introduced declaring that all dentists had to pass an exam and join a national register. The first person to register was John Tomes (1815–1895), who was knighted for his contributions to the profession.

RIGHT TOOLS FOR THE JOB

If you look after your teeth, toothache and false teeth may not come into the equation. Modern technology helps by providing more opportunities to save teeth and keep them healthy.

Toothbrushes

The Chinese claim to have invented the first bristle toothbrush in the 1400s; bristles from the necks of Siberian boars were attached to a bone or bamboo handle. The first toothbrushes to be sold in England, however, were made of cow bone handles and horse or pig hair bristles in the 1780s. In 1930, with the invention of nylon, artifical bristles were used for the first time.

Drills

Before the first clockwork drill was invented by British dentist George Harrington in 1864, dentists used files and chisels to remove tooth decay. In 1872, American dentist James B. Morrison (1829-1917) developed a foot-operated drill which worked like sewing machines of the time and could efficiently remove tooth decay. With the advent of electric drills later in the 1870s and air turbine drills in the 1950s, things became faster and less traumatic for patients.

Toothpaste and Mouthwashes

For thousands of years, people have used toothpaste and mouthwashes to freshen breath, keep teeth white, and clean teeth and gums, but it hasn't always been minty fresh. A Chinese recommendation from 2700BCE was to rinse your mouth with child's urine! The ancient Romans used more palatable things to rinse, such as wine, honey oil or beer.

False Teeth

False teeth are far from a modern invention – ox teeth held together with gold bands from around 700BCE were found in Italy. By the 1600s, some people inserted false teeth made from walrus, elephant or even hippo ivory! Later, false teeth were made from porcelain, but it wasn't until the development of vulcanite from the 1860s and then acrylic dentures from the 1930s that false teeth became more successful.

WARTIME INNOVATIONS

Wars always cause terrible injuries and many deaths. But they also force medical professionals to develop new treatments and practices rapidly to cope with enormous challenges. It is because of this that the Greek doctor Hippocrates described war as the best place for surgeons to train. Innovative medicines, surgical techniques, equipment and organisational ideas that started in wartime often go on to help the wider population.

1803–1815 NAPOLEONIC WARS

Dominique Jean Larrey (1766-1842), a French surgeon in Napoleon's army, first set up the 'triage' priority system (from the French word for 'to sort' or 'to select'): wounded soldiers were sorted into categories to decide how serious their injuries were.

Those with minor injuries could be treated quickly and go back to fight. Those with major injuries would be treated and recover over time. If casualties were so badly injured that they would not survive, sadly they did not receive treatment.

1853–1856 CRIMEAN WAR

This was the first British military campaign to use **anaesthesia** in the form of chloroform (see pages 40–41).

1899–1902 SECOND BOER WAR

The British Army took nine X-ray units to South Africa, making use of Röntgen's recent discovery (see page 22), so that they could find shrapnel in wounds more easily.

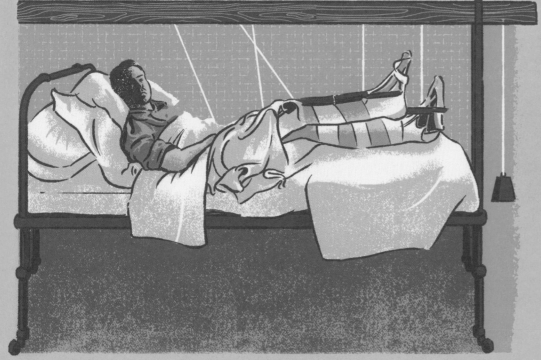

1914–1918 FIRST WORLD WAR

The introduction of the Thomas splint, an easy-to-use device that held a patient's leg totally still, saved thousands of lives and is still used today. It meant fewer amputations were needed, and therefore fewer deaths from infection.

In 1914, it was discovered that adding sodium citrate to blood prevented clotting, so, for the first time, blood could be stored on ice for up to 26 days, sent to where it was needed, and used later. Portable **transfusion** kits for use in battle were designed and the first blood banks were set up.

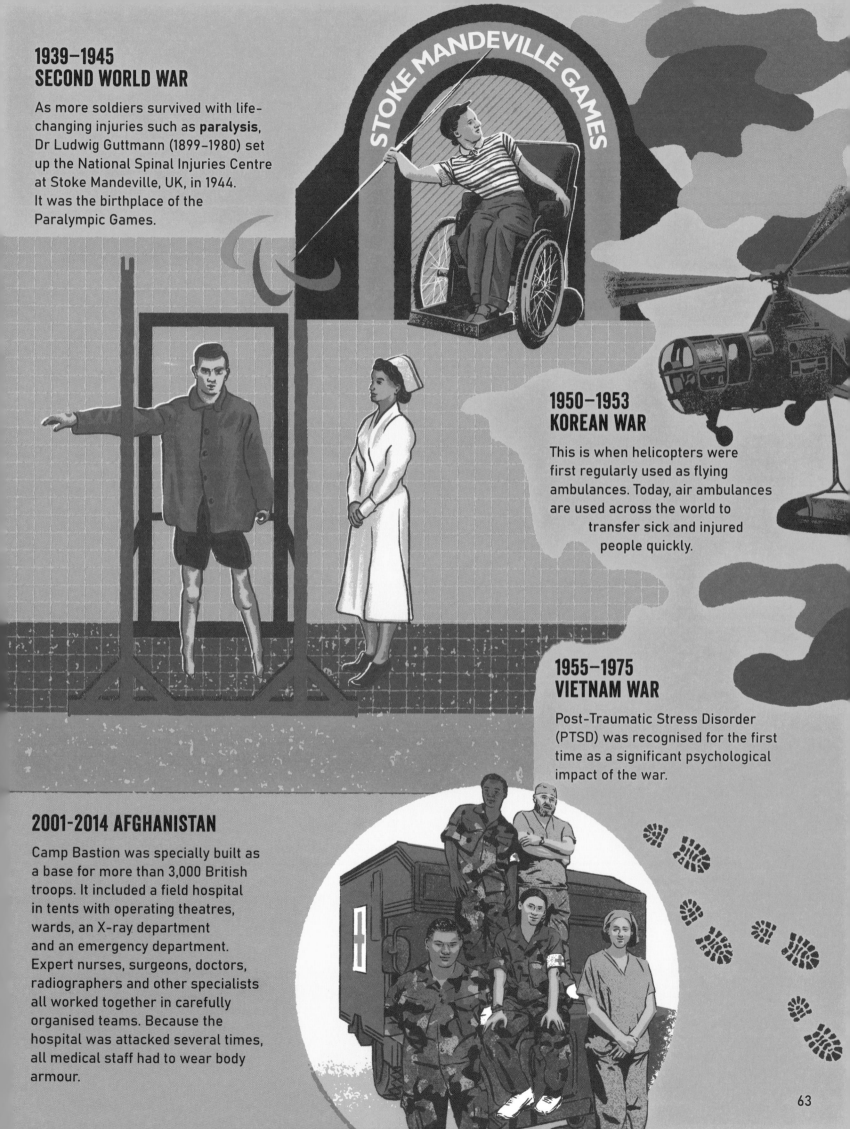

**1939–1945
SECOND WORLD WAR**

As more soldiers survived with life-changing injuries such as **paralysis**, Dr Ludwig Guttmann (1899–1980) set up the National Spinal Injuries Centre at Stoke Mandeville, UK, in 1944. It was the birthplace of the Paralympic Games.

STOKE MANDEVILLE GAMES

**1950–1953
KOREAN WAR**

This is when helicopters were first regularly used as flying ambulances. Today, air ambulances are used across the world to transfer sick and injured people quickly.

**1955–1975
VIETNAM WAR**

Post-Traumatic Stress Disorder (PTSD) was recognised for the first time as a significant psychological impact of the war.

2001-2014 AFGHANISTAN

Camp Bastion was specially built as a base for more than 3,000 British troops. It included a field hospital in tents with operating theatres, wards, an X-ray department and an emergency department. Expert nurses, surgeons, doctors, radiographers and other specialists all worked together in carefully organised teams. Because the hospital was attacked several times, all medical staff had to wear body armour.

TRANSFORMING NURSING THROUGH WAR

Nurses have a very long history of caring for the sick and looking after babies, children and older people. For centuries, however, they often had poor reputations and were accused of being drunk, too old or even too ignorant to be trusted! Apart from caring in the home, nurses worked at military hospitals. But nursing was transformed into a profession from the 1800s, prompted largely by the actions of British women during the Crimean War (1853-56) and American nurses during the Civil War (1861-65).

THE LADY WITH THE LAMP

Florence Nightingale (1820-1910) is probably the most famous nurse in history. Despite her family disapproving of her chosen career as a nurse, she trained in Germany before starting work in London. In 1854, Sydney Herbert, Secretary of State for War, asked her to organise a team of women to travel to the Scutari hospital in Constantinople, Turkey, to nurse soldiers wounded in the Crimean War. The hospital conditions were shocking, with one army surgeon describing the wards as being as muddy as a country road! More soldiers died from diseases they caught in the hospital than from their battlefield wounds. Nightingale was incredibly organised and worked hard to transform the situation. She became famous back in Britain with newspaper reports of the 'lady with the lamp' following her nightly routine of checking her patients.

Florence devoted the rest of her life to improving nursing and championing better training and higher standards for hospitals. This led to the establishment of the nursing school at St Thomas' Hospital in London and 'Nightingale' wards, which ensured good ventilation and an organised layout, transforming conditions for hospital patients. These ideas spread around the world. Around 2,000 volunteer nurses had served during the American Civil War, and in the 1870s, the first three nurse training schools were established in the US, inspired by Nightingale's recommendations.

MARY SEACOLE

Another famous nurse who travelled to the Crimea in 1855 was Mary Seacole (1805-1881). She told her story in *The Wonderful Adventures of Mrs Seacole in Many Lands*, published in 1857. She gained her nursing knowledge from her Jamaican mother, who treated many British officers and their families in Jamaica, drawing on Afro-Caribbean medical traditions. Mary herself nursed British soldiers in Jamaica and cholera patients in Panama before travelling to England to offer her services to the Crimean War. When she was turned down by officials, she instead went to the Crimea independently and opened 'the British Hotel' there to supply food, drink and care for soldiers; she also treated the wounded on the battlefield.

A NURSING PROFESSION

From the late 1880s, nurses were recruited to care for soldiers on campaigns around the world. In the First World War, thousands of nurses, many of them volunteers, worked across battlefields and on hospital ships. Nurses have continued to serve alongside soldiers and military colleagues in all major wars and humanitarian activities.

Like so many health professionals today, nurses have often travelled around the world for work, not just for military service. In Britain, many came to take up jobs in the new National Health Service, especially from Commonwealth countries. Today, nurses are highly qualified members of the healthcare team, working in surgeries, hospitals and clinics and visiting patients' homes. The profession has come a long way from its poor reputation in history.

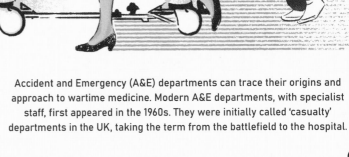

Accident and Emergency (A&E) departments can trace their origins and approach to wartime medicine. Modern A&E departments, with specialist staff, first appeared in the 1960s. They were initially called 'casualty' departments in the UK, taking the term from the battlefield to the hospital.

PENICILLIN

Before the discovery of antibiotics, people often died from bacterial diseases such as pneumonia or from infections. Although mould had been used for centuries to treat infected wounds, it took the urgent need to keep soldiers healthy in the Second World War to turn penicillin – discovered in 1928 – into a wonder drug in the 1940s.

A CHANCE DISCOVERY

In September 1928, Dr Alexander Fleming (1881–1955), a scientist at St Mary's Hospital in London, found mould growing on a petri dish in which he had been investigating bacteria. In the area surrounding the mould, the bacteria had been killed. Fleming's research found that juice from this mould – which he named penicillin – was poisonous to many types of bacteria. Believing it was nearly impossible to turn this discovery into an effective medicine, Fleming moved on to other projects.

1. *Penicillium* mould naturally produces the antibiotic penicillin. In the 1940s, scientists found that mould from rotting melons produced six times more penicillin than Fleming's original sample.

OXFORD RESEARCH

A team of scientists working in Oxford in the 1930s, led by Australian Howard Florey (1898–1968) and German-born Ernst Chain (1906–79), revisited Fleming's work. It took three years to crack the challenge of creating pure penicillin, but it was immediately successful on infected mice. The problem was how to produce enough penicillin to carry out tests on humans. Penicillin had to be extracted from a fermenting broth of mould, and baths, bedpans and milk churns were all used to produce only tiny amounts. Eventually, Norman Heatley (1911–2004), one of the team members, designed a special vessel and a team of six 'penicillin girls' worked full time to extract the 'mould juice'.

2. To produce enough penicillin to treat patients, scientists used deep fermentation tanks and mixed the mould broth with corn steep liquor, a liquid high in sugars and other substances that increased the growth of *Penicillium*.

The first patient was treated in 1941. It was Albert Alexander, a policeman who had cut his face pruning roses. Although the penicillin made him better, sadly there was not enough of it for a full recovery and he died five days later.

AMERICAN MASS PRODUCTION

Although penicillin could save lives, during the Second World War there were no British businesses able to take on the massive task of producing it. Instead, Florey and Heatley flew to America to try to persuade pharmaceutical companies to mass-produce the drug. When the US joined the war in December 1941, it was clear that penicillin could be vital to keep their soldiers healthy and able to fight. With government support, around 20 American companies worked together to produce enough supplies for all the American troops and their allies.

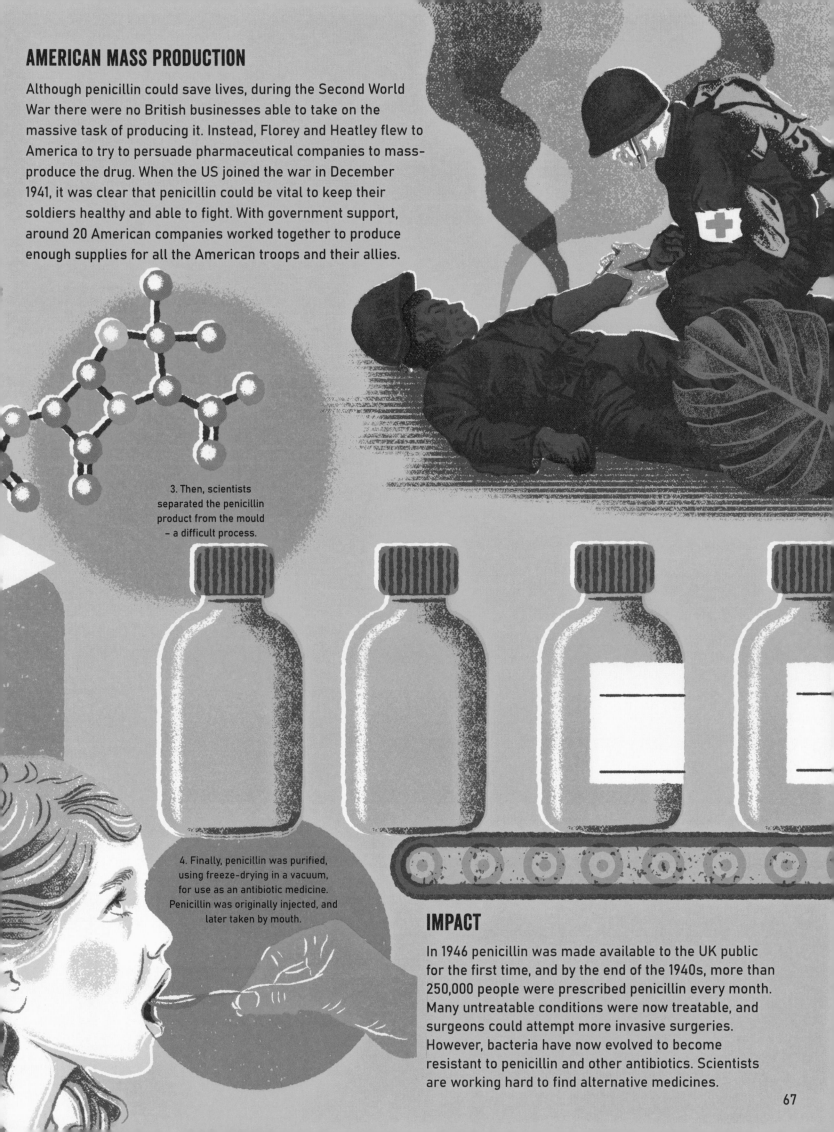

3. Then, scientists separated the penicillin product from the mould – a difficult process.

4. Finally, penicillin was purified, using freeze-drying in a vacuum, for use as an antibiotic medicine. Penicillin was originally injected, and later taken by mouth.

IMPACT

In 1946 penicillin was made available to the UK public for the first time, and by the end of the 1940s, more than 250,000 people were prescribed penicillin every month. Many untreatable conditions were now treatable, and surgeons could attempt more invasive surgeries. However, bacteria have now evolved to become resistant to penicillin and other antibiotics. Scientists are working hard to find alternative medicines.

KEEPING WELL FAR FROM HOME

If you are travelling into unfamiliar or dangerous conditions with no outside help, making plans to keep healthy and deal with emergencies is extremely important. While you might pack a first aid kit when you go on holiday, ships' surgeons and explorers in the past also needed to ensure they planned for every scenario.

SHIPS' SURGEONS

Whether for trade or battle, travelling by ship around the world could be a dangerous business. A ship's surgeon was responsible for carrying out emergency operations, including amputations, pulling out rotten teeth and even cutting the crew's hair! English military surgeon John Woodall (1570-1643) published *The Surgeon's Mate* in 1617 to advise ships' surgeons on medical treatments while at sea. It includes information about treating gunshot wounds, the plague and **gangrene**. He also suggested eating citrus fruits more than a century before Scottish doctor James Lind (1716-1794) confirmed that they prevented **scurvy**.

'TABLOID' FIRST-AID
FOR ALL EMERGENCIES

BRITISH
ANTARCTIC EXPEDITION
1910
BURROUGHS WELLCOME & CO
LONDON

A surgeon's chest found in the shipwreck of the Tudor *Mary Rose*, which sank in 1545, included ointments and spatulas. Archaeologists also recovered a feeding bottle probably used for sailors too injured to feed themselves.

RISKY EXPEDITIONS

European explorers faced many medical challenges as they travelled into exotic territory. Rather than turn to the local people's expertise, they often took medicine chests with familiar remedies from home. British explorers, including Captain Robert Scott (1868-1912) in Antarctica, were supplied with medicine chests made by Burroughs Wellcome (see page 31). Their innovative Tabloid pills compressed medicines into tiny tablet form and were ideal for explorers.

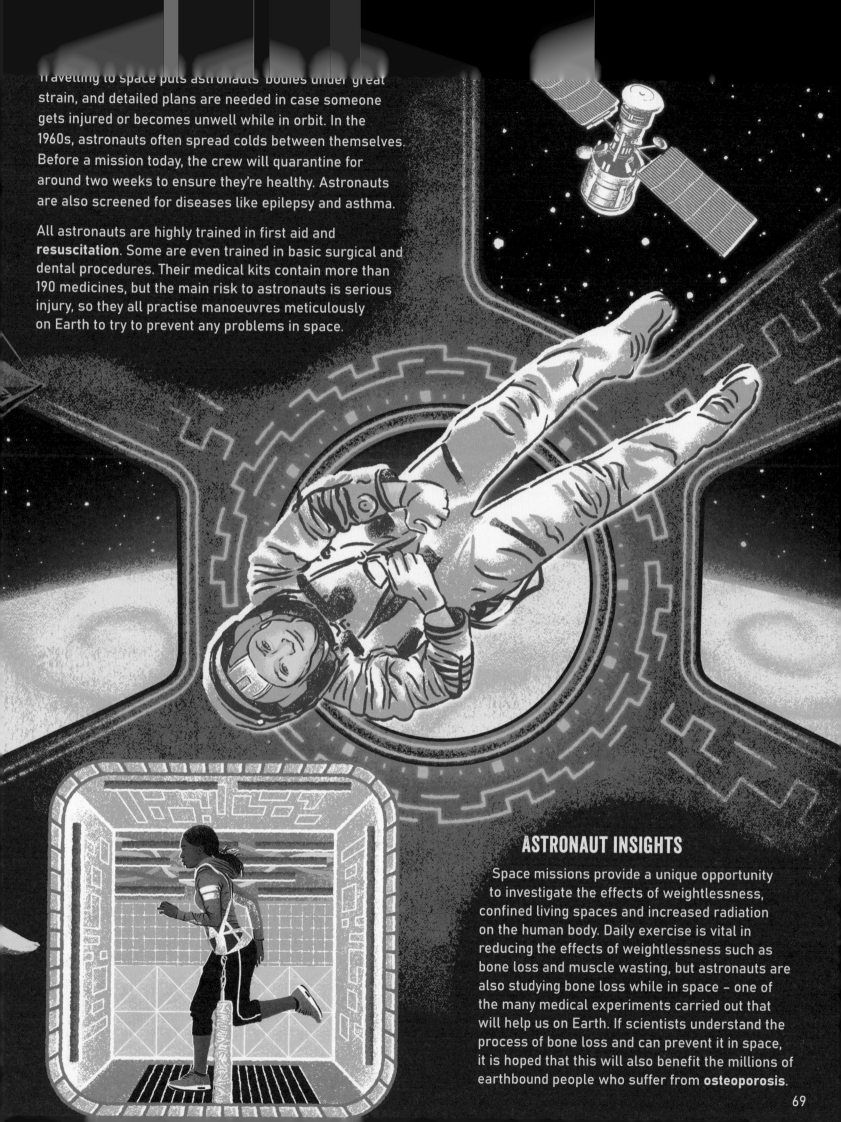

Travelling to space puts astronauts' bodies under great strain, and detailed plans are needed in case someone gets injured or becomes unwell while in orbit. In the 1960s, astronauts often spread colds between themselves. Before a mission today, the crew will quarantine for around two weeks to ensure they're healthy. Astronauts are also screened for diseases like epilepsy and asthma.

All astronauts are highly trained in first aid and **resuscitation**. Some are even trained in basic surgical and dental procedures. Their medical kits contain more than 190 medicines, but the main risk to astronauts is serious injury, so they all practise manoeuvres meticulously on Earth to try to prevent any problems in space.

ASTRONAUT INSIGHTS

Space missions provide a unique opportunity to investigate the effects of weightlessness, confined living spaces and increased radiation on the human body. Daily exercise is vital in reducing the effects of weightlessness such as bone loss and muscle wasting, but astronauts are also studying bone loss while in space – one of the many medical experiments carried out that will help us on Earth. If scientists understand the process of bone loss and can prevent it in space, it is hoped that this will also benefit the millions of earthbound people who suffer from **osteoporosis**.

D.I.Y. MEDICINE

Throughout history, scientists and doctors have gone to great lengths to test new medicines and techniques. Some have been so determined to prove their theories that they have put themselves at great risk, for example by drinking infected vomit! While they might have had a lot to lose personally, these professionals felt that their experiments had the potential to save lives, and many did just that.

PROVING A POINT: YELLOW FEVER

American doctor Stubbins Ffirth (1784-1820) wanted to prove that yellow fever was not contagious. His early experiments on animals hadn't worked, so he switched to experimenting on himself. Revoltingly, he poured fresh black vomit from an infected patient into cuts in his arm, then into his eye, and then he drank it! He remained well, proving that yellow fever is not spread through vomit.

CURIOUS ABOUT CURARE

Used by **indigenous** South Americans to poison their hunting blowpipe darts, the plant-based substance curare had fascinated European scientists for centuries. In 1947, American doctor Scott Smith wanted to test its anaesthetic effects. His colleagues used it to paralyse his body slowly, and then pricked him with pins. He showed them he could still feel pain throughout by blinking and wiggling his fingers. His experiment demonstrated that although curare was a very effective muscle relaxant, it needed to be combined with a painkiller.

SOLVING STOMACH BUGS

Most doctors did not believe that bacteria could live in the acid of the stomach, let alone cause ulcers or cancer. Australian doctor Barry Marshall (born 1951) wanted to prove his colleagues wrong. In 1984, he swallowed *Helicobacter* bacteria to test his theory. Marshall became ill and proved that bacteria can cause both **gastritis** and ulcers. Taking this risk meant that he helped millions of people as both conditions can now be treated with antibiotics. Marshall shared the Nobel Prize in 2005.

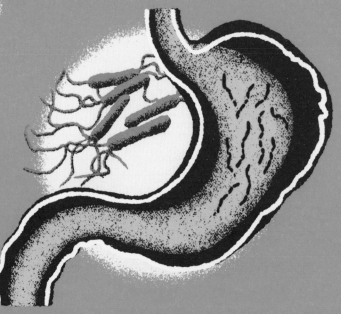

THE FIRST CARDIAC CATHETERISATION

In 1929, German doctor Werner Forssmann (1904–1979) secretly threaded a **catheter** through a **vein** in his arm into the right **atrium** of his heart – a risky move, as the effect of this procedure was unknown. Forssmann hoped to use this technique to measure blood pressure, or to deliver medicine or dyes to the heart safely... but would it be worth it? Although a triumph, Forssman faced disciplinary action for his self-experimentation and the damage to his reputation led him to leave heart medicine entirely. To his great astonishment, he later won the Nobel Prize.

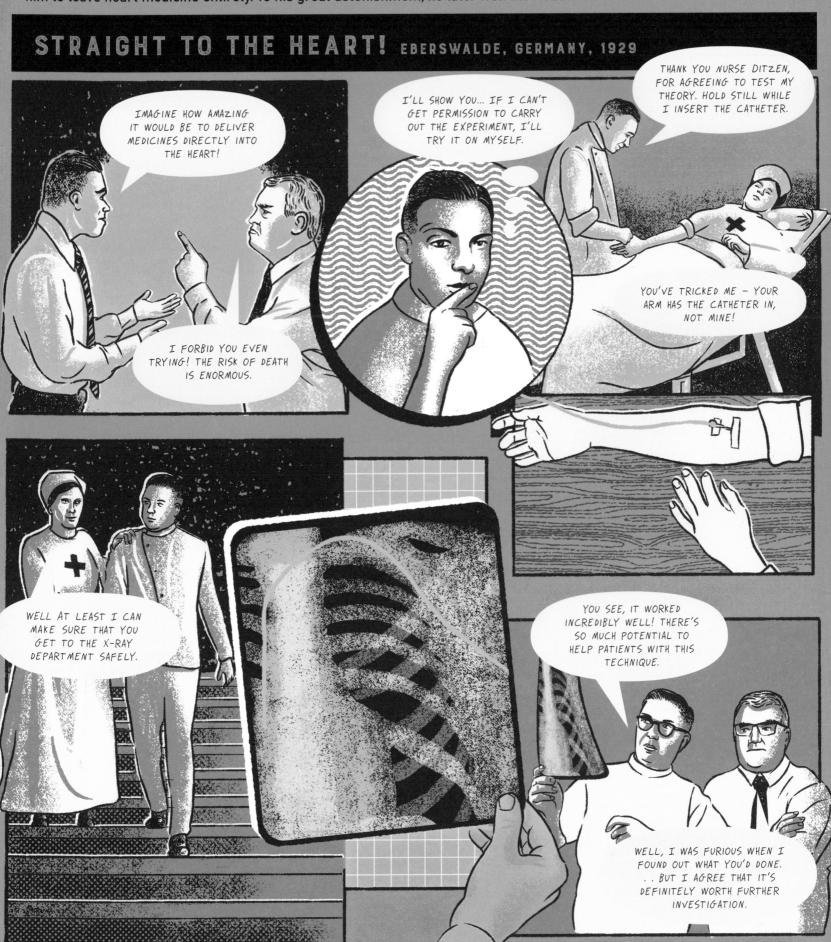

CHRONIC DISEASE

While many chronic diseases have ancient origins, medical understanding of their causes has changed enormously. As treatments and our living conditions have improved, life expectancy has too, meaning that patients and medical professionals have found new ways of treating and living with long-term, or chronic, illness.

ASTHMA

Asthma is a lung disorder that causes airways to swell and produce lots of mucus. It was described and treated by the ancient Greeks, with remedies including medicinal plants like hyssop, drinking animal blood or eating fox lungs! Today, the breathing difficulties of asthmatic people can be treated effectively with inhalers that use medicines to relax their muscles and open up their airways.

Incredibly, one asthma treatment in the 1900s was smoking cigarettes, to get a medicinal plant chemical from Datura leaves into a patient's lungs!

EPILEPSY

Epilepsy is a condition where sudden bursts of electrical activity in the brain cause fits or seizures. It was known historically as 'the falling disease', and epileptic seizures were often seen as mysterious or caused by supernatural forces. Our modern understanding of epilepsy builds on knowledge about electrical impulses in our nervous system and brain. More than a thousand years ago, Islamic doctor Ibn Sina (980-1037) seems to have been on the right track when he suggested holding an electric ray fish to an epileptic patient's forehead! By the 1860s, British physician John Hughlings Jackson (1835-1911) proposed that epileptic seizures were caused by an overwhelming discharge of energy from the nerves to the muscles. In 1929, German psychiatrist Hans Berger (1873-1941) invented the electroencephalograph (EEG) to measure the brain's electrical activity. Doctors still use EEGs today to diagnose epilepsy. There are around 50 million people living with the condition worldwide, who mainly manage their symptoms with medication.

EEG caps, or nets, are fitted with lots of electrodes which connect with the patient's scalp. They measure the electrical charges emitted by the brain.

DIABETES

Diabetes has a long history. Its full name, *diabetes mellitus*, means 'to pass through, sweetened with honey', because a diabetic person's urine is sweet. Today, we recognise that diabetes is caused when a hormone called **insulin** is missing or in low supply, so it can't perform its job of regulating blood sugar levels. The only early treatment for diabetes was to put patients on a very strict diet with no carbohydrates. A series of discoveries from the late 1800s, however, pointed towards an explanation for the condition, and the subsequent introduction of a daily injection of insulin to manage blood sugar meant that people with diabetes could live very different lives from those of their diabetic ancestors.

1869

A key discovery

German scientist Paul Langerhans (1847-1888) discovered that cells produce insulin.

1889

The importance of the pancreas

Oskar Minkowski (1858-1931) and Josef von Mering (1849-1908) showed that removing a dog's **pancreas** caused it to suffer from diabetes. They concluded that the pancreas was the important organ in controlling blood sugar levels.

1906

Pancreatic islets

Lydia DeWitt (1859-1928) isolated a cluster of cells from the pancreas, known as the islets of Langerhans. She discovered that they secreted a substance that helped the body to turn carbohydrates into energy.

1909

New terminology

Jean De Meyer (1878-1934) suggested the secretions be named 'insuline' – from the Latin word for island.

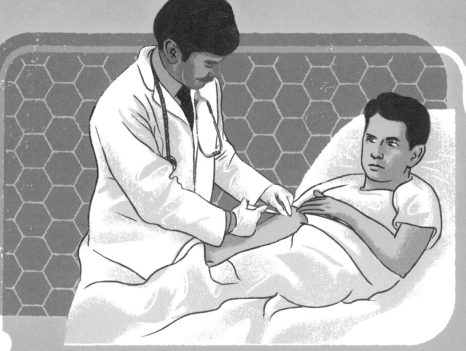

1922

Life-changing breakthrough

In Toronto, Canada, 14-year-old diabetic patient Leonard Thompson was the first person to receive insulin. The scientific team of Frederick Banting (1891-1941), John Macleod (1876-1935), James Collip (1892-1965) and Charles Best (1899-1978) had successfully purified the extract from dogs and cows.

1960S

New methods

Insulin was routinely extracted from cows and pigs, but from the 1960s scientists developed **synthetic** versions that could be manufactured.

1970S

Affordable treatment

Developments in the 1970s, led by German scientist Axel Ullrich (born 1943), cloned human genes to produce insulin which made treatment much cheaper. Today, nearly all insulin users inject human insulin rather than a product derived from animals.

TRANSPLANTS

Until recent history, if part of your body failed to work properly or was damaged beyond repair, your options would be very limited and even life-threatening. Replacing a failing internal organ like the heart or kidney is an incredibly challenging medical procedure for doctors and surgeons. It also depends on the generosity of donors and their families to donate their organs to help others.

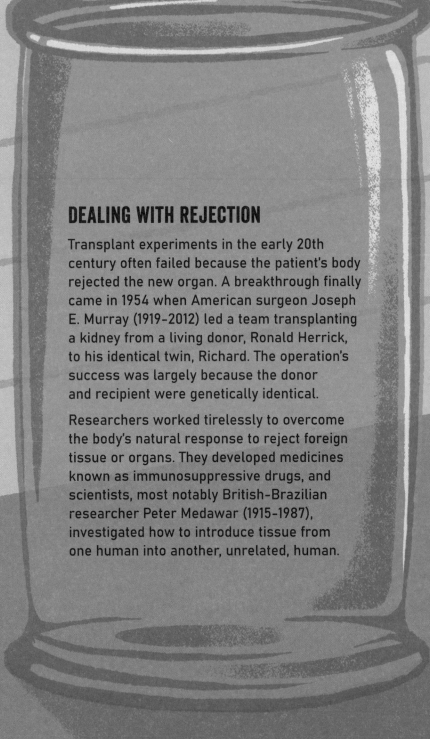

DEALING WITH REJECTION

Transplant experiments in the early 20th century often failed because the patient's body rejected the new organ. A breakthrough finally came in 1954 when American surgeon Joseph E. Murray (1919-2012) led a team transplanting a kidney from a living donor, Ronald Herrick, to his identical twin, Richard. The operation's success was largely because the donor and recipient were genetically identical.

Researchers worked tirelessly to overcome the body's natural response to reject foreign tissue or organs. They developed medicines known as immunosuppressive drugs, and scientists, most notably British-Brazilian researcher Peter Medawar (1915-1987), investigated how to introduce tissue from one human into another, unrelated, human.

BYPASSING THE HEART

The invention of the heart-lung machine by American couple John and Mary Gibbon made open-heart surgery possible in 1953, and later ensured that heart transplants could be considered. Still vitally important today, the machine takes over the functions of the heart and lungs by adding oxygen to the patient's blood and pumping it around their body.

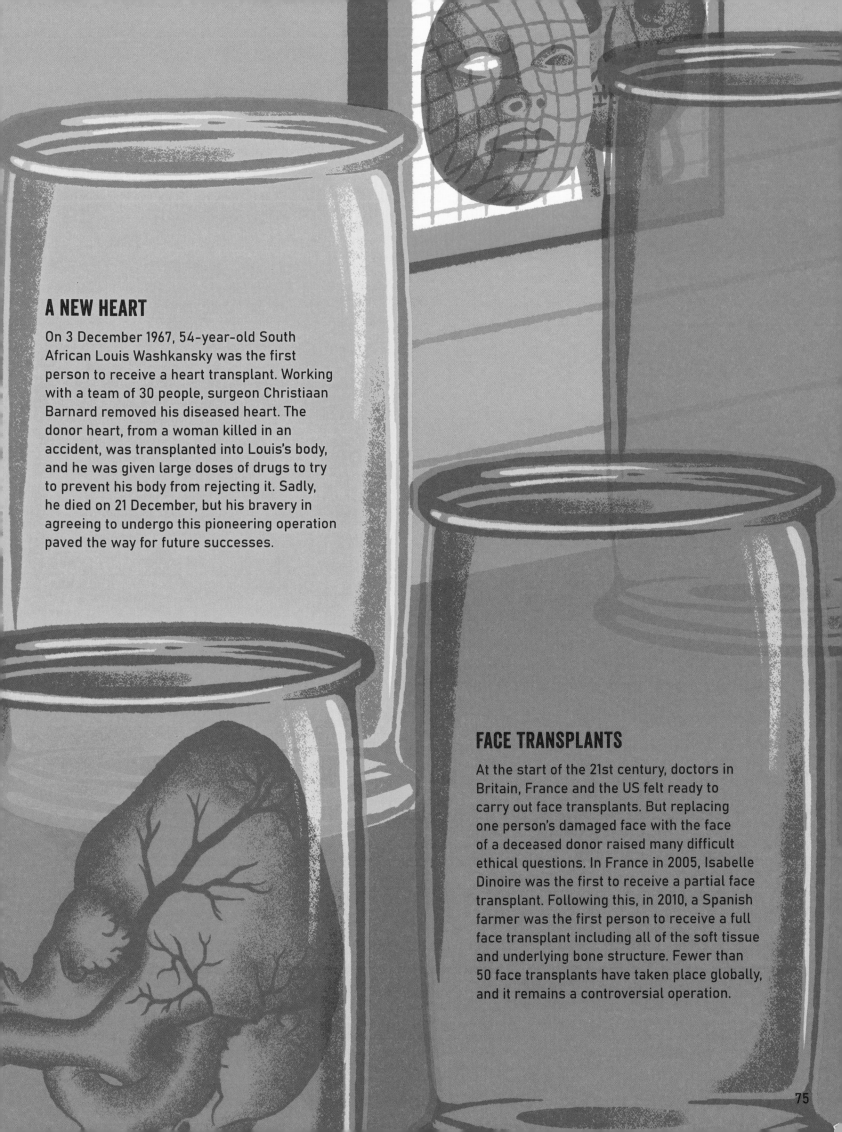

A NEW HEART

On 3 December 1967, 54-year-old South African Louis Washkansky was the first person to receive a heart transplant. Working with a team of 30 people, surgeon Christiaan Barnard removed his diseased heart. The donor heart, from a woman killed in an accident, was transplanted into Louis's body, and he was given large doses of drugs to try to prevent his body from rejecting it. Sadly, he died on 21 December, but his bravery in agreeing to undergo this pioneering operation paved the way for future successes.

FACE TRANSPLANTS

At the start of the 21st century, doctors in Britain, France and the US felt ready to carry out face transplants. But replacing one person's damaged face with the face of a deceased donor raised many difficult ethical questions. In France in 2005, Isabelle Dinoire was the first to receive a partial face transplant. Following this, in 2010, a Spanish farmer was the first person to receive a full face transplant including all of the soft tissue and underlying bone structure. Fewer than 50 face transplants have taken place globally, and it remains a controversial operation.

PROSTHETICS

If you are born with part of your body missing, develop a disability from an illness or injury, an artificial replacement or prosthesis can be the key to an independent life. Prostheses have a surprisingly long history; 3,000 years ago, an ancient Eqyptian priest called Ankhefenmut had a false toe! People who need prosthetics have helped experts to overcome the technical challenges involved in inventing replacements for human limbs. Recent technology has meant prostheses have come on in leaps and bounds – literally!

EARLY FALSE LEGS

European manuscripts and books from the 1200s onwards show us that some people used simple wooden prosthetic legs fixed below their knee, perhaps following battle injuries or because of **leprosy**. French military surgeon Ambroise Paré (1510–1590) was one of the first to publish designs for artificial arms and legs in 1579. Having seen how deeply amputation affected his patients, he began inventing replacement limbs that were inspired by real joints, for example with a knee that bent.

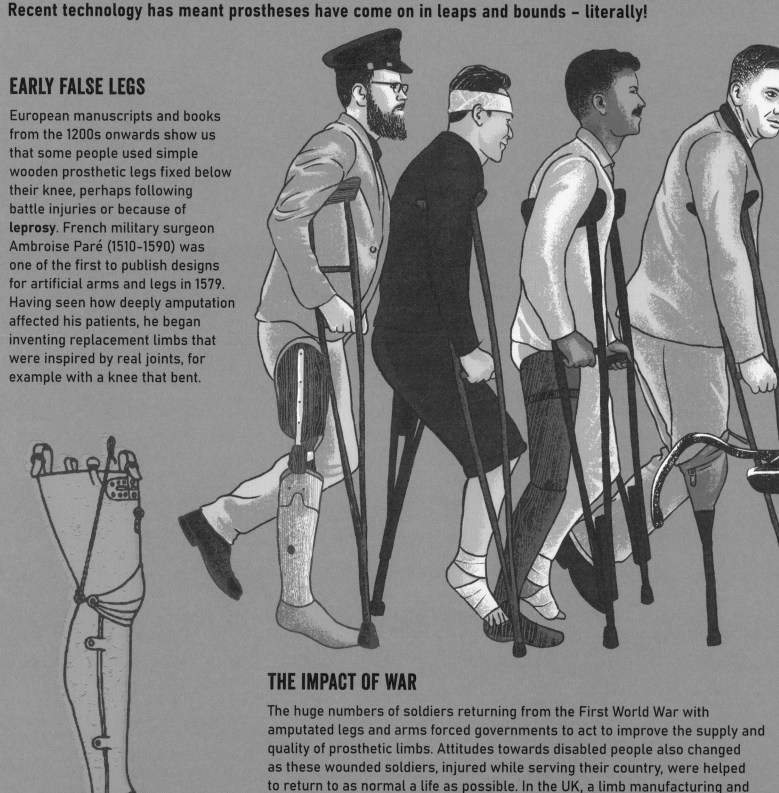

THE IMPACT OF WAR

The huge numbers of soldiers returning from the First World War with amputated legs and arms forced governments to act to improve the supply and quality of prosthetic limbs. Attitudes towards disabled people also changed as these wounded soldiers, injured while serving their country, were helped to return to as normal a life as possible. In the UK, a limb manufacturing and fitting centre at Queen Mary's Hospital, Roehampton, was established in 1915. Some veterans even trained to become limb makers themselves.

HIGH-TECH PROSTHETICS

Recent technology has revolutionised prosthetic limbs, although these developments can be very expensive. Using cosmetic silicone as an outer layer means they can be extremely lifelike and even include hair and freckles. Inventors have harnessed computer technology and robotics to allow patients to use their own thoughts to control the movement of the limb. In-built computers can even send sensations from the limb back to the user.

BOLD BLADES

Paralympians are probably the most well-known users of artificial legs. Their highly decorated blades, first invented in the 1970s by American amputee Van Phillips (born 1954), were inspired by kangaroos and cheetahs. They are specially designed for speed and spring but make no attempt to look like a human leg. High-profile athletes have changed attitudes towards disability; prosthetics are no longer something to hide away.

TACKLING FUTURE CHALLENGES

While we have come a long way, there's no doubt that everyone involved in health and medicine will continue to face challenges in the future. Inevitably, there will be difficult decisions, dead ends and tragic events – but also amazing breakthroughs – as humans continue to grapple with their complicated bodies and the conditions that they encounter. With inspiration from history coupled with cutting-edge technology to revolutionise treatments, researchers and practitioners will continue to meet challenges head-on.

LOOKING BACK TO MOVE FORWARD

Scientists looking for inspiration for new medicines have joined forces with historians, especially when it comes to treating hospital superbugs. International research teams have had exciting successes: a 10th-century Anglo-Saxon remedy for eye infections killed a range of microbes including **MRSA**; and honey and the pollen it contains is suggesting promising leads for future antibiotics. Researchers are also reinvestigating existing medicinal plants, including aspirin from willow, and artemisinin from wormwood, to look for potential cancer treatments.

SUPERDRUGS VS SUPERBUGS

Since the discovery of penicillin, scientists have developed more than a hundred different types of antibiotic to treat diseases and infections. However, bacteria have become resistant to many of these medicines, and 'superbugs' such as **E-coli** are now extremely difficult to treat. We may return to a situation when common infections could kill people, especially in poorer countries or disaster zones, with diseases like typhoid now resistant to virtually all antibiotics.

CUTTING-EDGE TECHNOLOGY

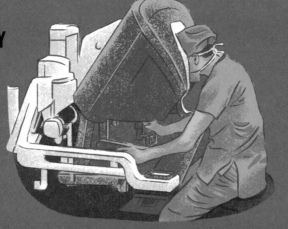

Inventors have created robots that allow human surgeons to operate from afar, whether on the battlefield or in space. By viewing 3D images of the inside of the patient's body, taken by the robot's tiny **endoscopic camera**, surgeons use a console that translates their hand movements into smaller precise movements of the robot's surgical instruments. Robot surgeons are incredibly expensive and human surgeons need to develop specialist expert skills to use them, but they are extremely accurate, reduce any natural tremor in a surgeon's hand and allow humans to operate from a safe position.

Developments in 3D printing have enabled pharmacist researchers to print tablets successfully. Personalised for individual patients, there are no transport costs and no impact on global warming. 3D printing is also being developed for implants, medical devices, bone or tissue. It might even be possible to 3D print organs for transplant in the future!

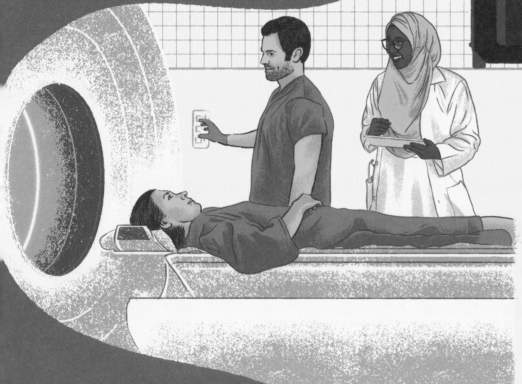

PERSONALISED MEDICINE

Now that scientists understand the human genetic code (see page 25), there is the potential to create personalised medicine that fits perfectly with each individual body's instruction manual or genome, avoiding side effects and ensuring that medicines work well for each unique patient. Scientists are also working towards new drug discoveries that precisely target the complex links between human bodies and disease. Pioneering developments have already started in patients with HIV, cystic fibrosis and rare childhood cancers.

SHARED AMBITIONS

Successful medical treatment in the future will depend on patients and professionals working together. This is true at an individual level with shared decisions about the best use for developing treatments. But it's also vitally important internationally. Ongoing public health measures are essential to prevent medical problems in the first place. Continued global partnerships should guarantee that it is not just rich countries that benefit from new advances. Our future shared ambition should be for everybody in the world to get the medicine and treatment that they need, wherever they are.

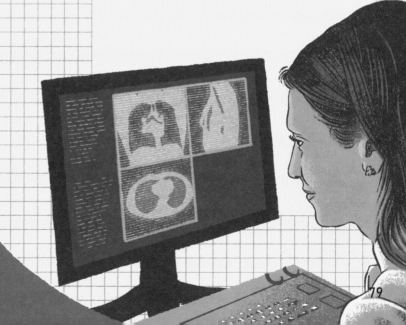

GLOSSARY

abscess a painful, swollen, infected collections of pus

AIDS (Acquired Immune Deficiency Syndrome) a number of potentially life-threatening infections that happen if the body's immune system has been severely damaged by the HIV virus

Alzheimer's disease the most common form of dementia, or decline in brain functioning

amputation the surgical removal of part of the body, like an arm or a leg

anaesthesia a state of controlled numbness or unconsciousness so that you don't feel pain during surgery

anatomy scientific study of the structure of human and animal bodies

anthrax a serious bacterial disease, sometimes passed to humans from sheep and cows

antibiotic a medicine used to treat or prevent some bacterial infections

antibody a protein in the blood that responds to a particular disease entering the body

antidote a medicine taken to act against a poison

antisepsis preventing the growth of micro-organisms that cause disease

apothecary in history, a person who prepared and sold medicines

archaeologist a person who studies history by excavating sites and analysing the evidence they find there

aseptic free from any micro-organisms that cause disease

atrium one of two spaces in the upper heart

Ayurveda a traditional Hindu system of medicine

bile a bitter fluid that is made by the liver, stored in the gall bladder and helps digestion; one of the ancient four humours

botulism now rare life-threatening condition caused by toxic bacteria

bronchitis an infection of the main airways of the lungs

catheter a flexible thin tube that can be put into the body, including the bladder or the heart

cholera a potentially fatal bacterial infection that causes extreme diarrhoea and dehydration

cloned when a copy is made using a fragment of DNA

colonised established control over a place and the people who lived there

constipation difficulty emptying the bowels

cuneiform an ancient writing system used in Mesopotamia and Persia

curator a person who works in museums and looks after historical collections

deficiency a lack of something, like vitamins in the body

diabetes a lifelong condition that causes a person's blood sugar level to become too high

diphtheria a highly contagious bacterial infection that mainly affects the nose and the throat

dysentery an infection of the intestines that causes diarrhoea containing blood or mucus

E-coli (Escherichia coli) a bacterium that lives in the intestines and can cause severe stomach cramps, diarrhoea and vomiting

endemic constantly present within a specific location

endoscopic camera using a long thin flexible tube with a light and camera at one end to look at organs inside the body without performing an operation

enzyme a protein that controls the chemical reactions in our bodies

epilepsy a condition where sudden bursts of electrical activity in the brain cause fits or seizures

flammable easily set on fire

fracture a broken bone

gangrene a serious condition where body tissue dies because the blood supply fails

gastritis a condition where the stomach lining is damaged and inflamed

gout a type of arthritis that causes severe joint pain

HIV (Human Immunodeficiency Virus) damages the immune system, making it hard for the body to fight infections and disease

hormone a chemical substance produced in the body that helps control how cells and organs do their work

immune system the body's defence against infections

immunity the ability of a person to keep themselves protected from a disease

indigenous originally belonging to a particular place

insulin a hormone that regulates blood sugar levels in the body

laxative something that stimulates the bowels to evacuate, to treat constipation

leprosy a contagious disease that affects the skin and nervous system, and can cause severe deformities

mania a mental health condition causing people to feel frenzied and overactive

measles a highly infectious viral illness, with a fever and rash

melancholy a sad feeling; in the past used to describe a medical condition like depression

MRSA (Methicillin-Resistant Staphylococcus Aureus) a type of bacterium that is resistant to several widely used antibiotics

mumps a contagious viral infection, with painful swellings at the side of the face

neurology the study of the nervous system

obstetrician a doctor who specialises in delivering babies and caring for pregnant women

osteoporosis a health condition that weakens bones

pancreas a small organ, located behind the stomach, that helps with digestion

pandemic a disease outbreak that spreads across a large region, or the whole world

paralysis the loss of the ability to move some or all of the body

parasite an organism that lives in, or on, another organism

pathogen a bacterium, virus or other organism that causes disease

pharmacist someone professionally qualified to prepare and dispense medicines

phlegm a thick sticky substance, especially produced during a cold; historically, one of the four bodily humours

physician a doctor, someone professionally qualified to practise medicine

physiologist an expert scientist in understanding how the body works

placebo a treatment with no medicinal ingredients

pneumonia a bacterial or viral infection that causes swelling in the lungs

polio now rare, a serious viral infection that can attack the nerves in the spine and brain, causing paralysis

prescription instructions written by a medical practitioner to give a patient medicine

psychiatry the study of mental illness, behaviours and emotions

quarantine putting a person or animal in isolation to prevent the spread of disease

rabies a rare, but very serious viral infection of the brain and nerves, usually caught from an infected animal

resuscitation the process of reviving someone who is unconscious

rickets a condition that affects bone development in children, usually caused by a lack of vitamin D or calcium

SARS (Severe Acute Respiratory Syndrome) caused by a coronavirus that gives people a very serious contagious form of pneumonia

scrofula a historical word for a type of tuberculosis that caused swollen neck glands

scurvy a disease caused by severe lack of vitamin C in a person's diet

sewage used water and human waste

synthetic made using chemical processes, often to copy a natural product

syphilis a bacterial infection, usually caught from sexual intercourse with an infected person

tetanus a serious but rare condition, caused by bacteria getting into a wound

tonsillitis an infection of the tonsils, at the back of the throat

toxin a poisonous substance

Traditional Chinese Medicine an ancient system of healthcare developed in China and still practised today

transfusion transferring blood or other fluids from one person to another

tuberculosis a bacterial infection that mainly affects the lungs

typhoid fever a highly contagious bacterial infection that affects many organs

Unani Tibb an ancient system of medicine practised in Central and South Asia

vaccine a substance that teaches the immune system to produce the right antibodies to attack infections

vein a tube in the body's blood circulation system

vivisection carrying out scientific tests on live animals

X-ray crystallography a scientific method to find out the atomic and molecular structure of a crystal using X-rays